HOW TO TALK TO A BROKER

JAY J. PACK

BARNES & NOBLE BOOKS
A DIVISION OF HARPER & ROW, PUBLISHERS
New York, Cambridge, Philadelphia, San Francisco
London, Mexico City, São Paulo, Sydney

This book is sold with the understanding that neither the Author nor the Publisher is engaged in rendering legal or financial services. Questions relevant to the practice of law or personal finance should be addressed to a member of those professions.

The Author and Publisher specifically disclaim any liability, loss, or risk, personal or otherwise, which is incurred as a consequence, directly or indirectly, of the use and application of any of the contents of this work.

Produced by Cloverdale Press Inc. 133 Fifth Avenue, New York, NY 10003

FIRST EDITION

Library of Congress Cataloging in Publication Data

Pack, Jay J.
  How to talk to a broker.

(The Smart money series)

  1. Brokers.   2. Investments.   I. Title.   II. Series.
HG4621.P33   1985   332.6'78   84-48413

ISBN 0-06-464099-X

85 86 87 88 89 10 9 8 7 6 5 4 3 2 1

CONTENTS

Introduction

Have you ever wondered how the rich get richer, and how their investments seem to grow by leaps and bounds, in good times and bad? The answer is quite simple—they know how to talk to their brokers.

Unfortunately, most of us feel rather timid or uncertain about talking to a broker. The world of the Big Board, Wall Street, commodities, REITS, and hedge funds may be a great mystery to us. We may feel we don't have enough money to be of interest to a broker, especially since he often seems too busy to talk with us—and when he *does*, many of us can't understand what he says!

But all that can be changed. This book can help you get over that hurdle by taking you directly into the world of the stockbroker and showing you how to speak his language.

Getting to Know a Broker for Fun and Profit

Brokers, you will soon discover, are valuable people to know. Good brokers have specialized training, experience, and knowledge in a complex and rapidly changing field. They can advise you about saving, investing, sheltering income, and protecting your hard-earned dollars. Often they make money for you—sometimes a lot of money. And they can always help put financial matters in proper perspective for you.

Twenty-five years as a Wall Street stockbroker have put me in contact with many new or nervous investors. But by working together, these people were able to overcome their fears of the market and turn into experienced investors. So can you. You can learn all about opening an account, building a portfolio, making the best use of zero coupon bonds, options, municipals, tax shelters—all the paraphernalia of the financial world. You can learn how to talk to a broker—in person and on the telephone—and how to get the most out of him.

1

More important this book will help you put your financial profile in order, even before you "walk in the door." You will learn how to determine your net worth and make a list of sound financial goals. You'll be prepared for the kinds of questions brokers ask potential clients at their first meeting, and you'll learn which questions to ask when shopping for the right firm and broker for you.

Making Investment Decisions

We are all accustomed to seeking professional help in such diverse areas as our physical health, our nutrition, and our psyches. Managing our money requires just as much qualified guidance. Because some brokers are better than others, your ability to select among them is crucial to your economic health.

To make sound financial decisions you have to do your homework first and think carefully about what you want to do. Most important, talk to your broker—and get him talking to you! From those dialogues wisdom and wealth may follow.

PART ONE

Before You Walk in the Door

Winning the Broker Hunt Game

Client:	*I'm so pleased with the way things have been going in my account. You certainly know how to pick stocks.*
Broker:	Thanks. I've been at it awhile. And we've been lucky.
Client:	*I know it's not all luck. Do you use a special method?*
Broker:	Not really. I try to pick medium-sized companies that are off the beaten track, and in your case, since you're looking for growth plus some income, this approach has worked well. Now let's take a few minutes and see what we can find for your IRA contribution this year.

Not everyone is fortunate enough to find such a good broker as this. But it's quite possible if you do your homework and win the broker hunt game.

How to Find a Broker

It's tough, of course, deciding which broker to go to. You don't want just any broker. You want someone special—someone who is adept at dealing with your particular needs and goals, someone who will listen carefully and then set up a program tailored just for you.

Until you start on your broker hunt, it may seem like an impossible task—after all, there are over 50,000 stockbrokers to choose from. How will you ever find the one best suited for you? And how can you conduct your search without spending endless hours?

It *is* possible to find a broker to suit your needs. It *will* take time and effort, however, and there are several ways to go about your broker hunt. *Don't* do what most new investors do—that is, walk

4

into a local brokerage office cold, without a referral. With or without an appointment, you will probably be assigned the first available account representative, whether or not he's the right one for you.

Most of the large brokerage firms would like to see you select your account representative in exactly this fashion. They offer the protective umbrella of their research, prestige, and advertising program so that you will feel comfortable and secure about your investments, while they sell you *their* products.

Picking a stockbroker shouldn't be like that at all. Select your broker as carefully as you would your family doctor. Doing a little advance research and preparation will prove valuable in the long run. Follow the steps outlined below, and within a short time you'll succeed in finding the right broker for your particular needs.

Step One

Use whatever contacts you already have. You may think you don't have any influential contacts, but that's probably quite untrue. Do you have a lawyer? An accountant? Tax accountants, who monitor the investment records of their clients, are often in a position to know of good stockbrokers. If you don't know of anyone, ask if your brother does, or a friend. Find out how successful your friend's broker has been, and then insist on a second endorsement.

Ask around at work. Who handles things like your company's pension fund or the president's portfolio? Get specific details on their performance. Have they at least keep pace with the Dow Jones Industrial Average? What is their specialty?

You may want to talk to your bank's trust officer, often an excellent source of information. He deals with many different brokers and knows which ones speculate, which ones are conservative, which ones have the best track records. Your banker may actually refer you to a specific broker to handle your investments.

You can even get recommendations at a party:

You: *Say, I've been meaning to ask you about your broker. I gather from what you've told me you're pretty pleased with him.*

Your Friend: I am, indeed. He's not a miracle worker, but I find him sound and conservative. He's even reachable and always seems to have time to explain what's going on

5

You:	*Can I have his name and phone number? I'd like to call him.*
Your Friend:	Sure, and if for any reason he can't handle your account, ask him if he can recommend someone else. I think you could trust him to give you a first-rate referral.
You:	*Thanks. I'll call him tomorrow morning.*
Your Friend:	Listen, just one word of advice—try to have your act together before you interview him. He'll need to know a lot of things like your income and what you're looking for.

Step Two

Read professional opinions on brokers. This approach will help you narrow your choice. You can turn to several publications for the names of specific brokers and firms.

Top ranking brokers are also the subject of articles in professional literature. Go to the library and look over last year's issues of several publications, especially *Financial World*, *Forbes*, *Money*, *Money Maker*, and *Barron's*. Fund managers, stockbrokers, and publishers of financial newsletters are described, interviewed, and often evaluated. Their past performance records are frequently included, as is a description of the route they took toward success. These are the men and women whom the editors and the financial community regard as successful.

The Wall Street Journal's weekly column "Heard on the Street" is filled with quotes from brokers, fund managers, and analysts, and you can use it as a never-ending source for names to consider. The *Journal's* reporters have a stable of reliable analysts and brokers they call upon regularly for news. If a firm has underwritten a new issue or come out with an interesting report on a "hot" industry or company, it will occasionally notify the *Journal*.

Use the *Journal* articles primarily for names and background information, and keep in mind that a discussion of specific stocks to buy generally appears in print *after* they have gone up in price.

The December issue of *Financial World* traditionally carries a listing of the year's top ten brokers. This feature is fertile territory for investors seeking names of successful brokers.

Step Three

Read advertisements in the financial pages of newspapers for brokerage firms. Restrict your responses to members of the New York Stock Exchange, with the exception of discount brokers (see chapter 13). Members of the NYSE are subject to strict regulation and surveillance. Then?

Step Four

Select the right broker for you. It's not always easy, or automatic, especially if you have only a small amount to invest. But it's certainly not impossible.

Once you have obtained the names of several brokers and thought about the type of firm best suited to you (read chapter 4), go shopping! Telephone the brokers on your list and, in addition to giving them your name, be certain to mention immediately who recommended them to you. Then indicate the approximate amount of money you have to invest at this time. (If at all possible, try to open your account with at least $1,000, keeping in mind that your broker's commission must be paid from the costs of any stock you buy.) You want to find a broker who is interested in helping clients within your income and net worth group.

If the brokers you call are not accepting new accounts right now, ask them to recommend another broker for you. You will find that competent but busy brokers are almost always happy to give you an honest referral to someone they really respect.

After you have made appointments to interview several brokers, take a half hour or so to prepare yourself for the meeting. Review the items we discuss in chapters 5 and 6, and take notes during the interviews. During your initial interview you should be able to discuss the following topics with a broker (we will explain each one in detail in chapters 2 and 3):

- Your net worth

- Your financial goals—roughly whether you are looking for long-term appreciation, immediate income, or tax-free returns

- Your appetite for taking financial risks

- Your feelings about a discretionary account (see chapter 7)—that is, one in which the broker makes all the buy-and-sell decisions and then acts upon them without your go-ahead

- Your possible inheritance
- Your position in the financial pyramid (see chapter 3)

The first five minutes with a broker might go something like this.

You: *I'd like to inquire about opening an account.*
Broker: What size account do you have in mind?

This is always the broker's first line of inquiry; he wants to know how much money he will have to work with. Your response could then be:

You: *I'm not sure. Can you describe the different types you offer?*

Here you are being a little clever and trying to draw out the broker. Eventually you will tell him how much you want to invest, but let him talk first. You want to hear what he has to say about his investment philosophy (whether it's conservative or daring), his approach to an investment of your size, and your financial goals.

During these first five minutes (or beforehand, while you are waiting to talk to a broker), many large firms ask prospective clients to fill out an information form, which supplies them with pertinent details about you and your finances.

After you've completed the form, you will speak with an account representative, who will give you an idea of the services offered by his firm:

Broker: Sure. We have a cash management account, which requires an initial deposit of $20,000. This combines our money fund, full checking privileges, and a debit card.* In addition, you can buy stock for cash or on margin using the same account.

You: *I'm not sure I want to start with that much.*
Broker: Then you can open an account for any amount and just buy stocks. That would be a regular account. You

---

* *Debit card:* No bills are sent as is the case with a regular credit card. Money is taken from (or debited) your account as soon as each charge is received, thus eliminating interest charges on late payments and some paperwork.

would earn interest on idle funds in our regular money market account and at the same time you can write checks for $500 or more. You have to have $1,000 to participate in the money fund, though.

You: *Does the regular account include a credit or debit card?*
Broker: No.

You: *Could I open an account for less than $1,000?*
Broker: Yes. That is handled by our special accounts department. If you leave your name and telephone number, I'll have someone call you.

This conversation actually took place in the metropolitan area office of one of the larger wirehouses (see page 33). It is quite typical given the situation—that the customer walked in without an appointment and was uncertain about how much to invest. You will note also that the broker used phrases such as "cash management account," "buy for cash or on margin," and "money market account." Unless you have learned the meaning of such terms (see chapter 3), the conversation will sail right by. Fortunately, you won't get caught like this if you read this book before your interview. But if you get confused, don't hesitate to ask questions.

Soon we will move on to the specific questions you should ask once you are in the door. But before we do, one last word of advice: Try to be as brief as possible and still cover the suggestions in this book. Keep your interview to a maximum of one hour. Suggest a second meeting or a phone call to handle questions not covered initially. Time is of the essence to a broker, especially during busy market hours. As a general rule, it is best to hold your meeting before or after the stock market is open (10 A.M. to 4 P.M. Eastern time).

DO'S

- Do your homework before interviewing any broker.

- Do write out your questions ahead of time. That way you will be sure you asked everything on your list.

- Do reach out for additional information. Get references and details. Find out what type of relationship your friend has with the broker he or she is recommending. Ask what the broker's best and worst points are.

- Insist on a face-to-face interview. Don't settle for a telephone conversation. Distrust and incompatibility are more likely to show up in person.

- Do ask tough questions, even if they seem combative.

- Do interview at least three brokers before making your final choice.

DON'TS

- Don't be a walk-in client. Make an appointment.

- Don't sign up with the first broker you meet.

- Don't settle for a broker who has not experienced both *bull* and *bear* markets.

- Don't respond to a cold phone call from a broker you never heard of.

- Don't use a "brilliant" broker if he makes you feel uncomfortable.

- Don't give your account to a broker who only handles much wealthier clients.

- Don't use a broker who promises to make you rich.

2 Doing Your Homework

Before we address the question of homework, take a moment to read the true experiences described below. You'll see why doing your homework is fun and profitable.

- Theresa L. inherited $8,500 from her uncle. She put it in her savings bank, where it was earning 5.25 percent. When she found the right broker, he was able to help her more than double her rate of return.

- Ralph B. and his wife, Sarah, through the help of their broker were able to buy $6,000 worth of zero coupon bonds which would take care of most of their two-year-old daughter's college education.

- Norman F. invested approximately $12,000 in a nationwide convenience food chain suggested by his broker. He bought 4,000 shares at $3 per share. It's now worth over $70,000.

Any professional does his best when he's armed with plenty of solid information. Your doctor needs to know where it hurts, how high your fever is, which drugs you are allergic to. And so it is with a broker. He needs to know if high taxes are hurting your bottom line, if you need more current income, if your earnings are erratic.

You can help him give you his best performance by preparing facts about your finances ahead of time—before you walk in the door. You need to know what your financial picture is now and what you want it to be ten or twenty years from now. Do you want to invest for immediate income, for long-term appreciation, for tax-free returns, or a combination of all three? A broker also needs to know your appetite for risk—how much you are comfortable with, and how much you are willing to assume.

So we come to the issue of homework. There are five assignments you must do in order to make that first meeting a success.

Determining Your Net Worth

After shaking your hand, the first question any broker will ask is, "How much are you prepared to invest?" (Or, at least, how much will you place on deposit with the firm?) He won't come right out and ask you to reveal your precise net worth, but you can be certain he's trying to guess at it from what you tell him. So, before your first visit, you should know the answer and then decide for yourself what details to share with him.*

Don't panic. You don't need an MBA to do the calculations. There are two simple steps involved in determining your net worth: adding up the value of all that you own (your assets), then subtracting the total of all your debts (liabilities). What's left over is your net worth. Hopefully, you'll have a positive number.

In order to get a clear picture of your present net worth, imagine that time stands still. Nothing moves. The clock stops ticking. Your next salary check, payable this Friday, hasn't been written. Now get a pencil and pad and keep track as you ask yourself:

- What is my checking account balance?

- What savings accounts or certificates of deposit do I have?

- What is the value of any property I own free and clear (house, boat, car)?

- What money is owed to me that I stand a good chance of collecting, and when?

- Do I have a retirement plan where I work? What is it worth to me today?

- Do I have an IRA or Keogh plan? What are they worth?

- What is the value of my life insurance if I cashed it in today?

- What is the value of any personal property I own, such as antiques, jewelry, stamps, coins, precious metals?

By the way, whether you ever visit a broker or not, it's smart to figure out what you're worth. It gives you a cumulative picture of what's happened to all the cash that's been passing through your hands since you started working. The shock may force you into setting up a sensible budget!

When all this is added up, subtract your debts, remaining mortgage payments, and any balances due on loans and credit cards. The result is your net worth. With this information, you and your broker can determine the right mixture of investments—whether you need to look for immediate income, long-term growth, or a little of both—and, given your net worth, what level of risk is appropriate.

YOUR NET WORTH

WHAT YOU OWN (Assets)

Date _____

CASH AND CASH EQUIVALENTS	DOLLAR AMOUNT
Cash on hand	_____
Cash in checking accounts	_____
Cash in savings accounts	_____
Life insurance cash value	_____
Savings bonds	_____
Money owed you	_____

PERSONAL PROPERTY	EST. MARKET VAULE
Household furnishings	_____
Valuables (furs, antiques, jewelry, etc.)	_____
Car, boat, tractor, etc.	_____
Misc.	_____

REAL ESTATE

Your house _____

Other properties _____

INVESTMENTS

Stocks _____

Bonds _____

Government securities _____

Other misc. investments _____

Equity interest in your business _____

Vested interest in pension or
profit-sharing plan _____

Keogh or IRA _____

YOUR NET WORTH
WHAT YOU OWE (Liabilities)

Date _____

CURRENT BILLS   DOLLAR AMOUNT

Current account balances _____

Credit cards _____

Utilities _____

Rent _____

Insurance premiums _____

Taxes _____

Other bills _____

AMOUNT OWED ON LOANS

Mortgage _____

Automobile loans _____

Personal loans _____

Installment loans _____

Life insurance loans _____

TAXES DUE _____

OTHER _____

YOUR NET WORTH

Date _____

TOTAL ASSETS _____

TOTAL LIABILITIES   *minus* _____

NET WORTH
(assets minus liabilities) _____

You may be pleasantly surprised at how much you're worth. Whether you are or not, though, this knowledge is the key to understanding your financial future and planning it with your broker.

Knowing Your Salary Expectations

Now you can release the hold on the clock and allow time to continue. Back to the real world of moving cars, noise, and people. The second question your broker will want to know the answer to is, "What is your present salary, and what are your salary expectations?" The picture generally looks like this for people who are just out of college and starting their careers:

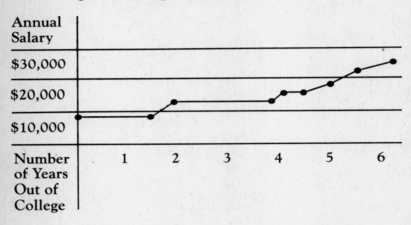

Or it may look more like this for those who are older and expecting to eventually slow down or go into retirement:

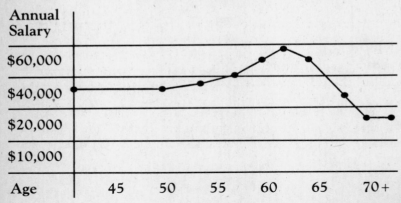

In either case, it is important for your broker to know your salary expectations. Without this information, he is unable to help you select suitable investments. (Naturally this information will remain confidential.) Why? Because most investments, in order to realize their full potential, should be tailored to the income level and age of the investor. For example, if you have an income between $15,000 and $20,000, too much investment risk is inappropriate because you need to protect your capital. On the other hand, if you have a high income, a tax shelter with a degree of risk may be a prudent move.

The following episode will explain what I mean. A few months ago, a young married couple, both lawyers, came into my office to talk about financial planning. They had recently been married and together had set a specific goal—to save enough for a down payment on a house. Most of their income was going to living expenses and paying off student loans. Actually, they had a negative net worth.

Their salary expectations, however, were extremely favorable. After covering their living expenses and a small amount of entertainment, they felt confident they could save $1,000 per month. I recommended they use a money market mutual fund, because at that time the interest rate was a healthy 10+ percent. This was the best vehicle for their savings; it paid high rates and kept their money liquid at the same time, ready to be moved into action when the right house became available. We figured out that after three years they would save nearly $42,000.

This couple's favorable salary expectations also helped them obtain a variable-rate mortgage with relative ease—even with a small down payment. After they purchased their house, a part of their rising salaries was sheltered from income tax by their mortgage interest payments, which were deductible.

Not all of us, of course, have such high salaries. But most people can put some money aside for an investment program, and this is our next piece of homework—namely, why and how we should budget for investing.

What I earn annually right now	$_____
What I expect to earn next year	$_____
What I expect to earn five years from now	$_____
My age	_____
Number of dependents	_____

Budgeting for Investing

Everyone hates a budget. Yet there's no way around the fact that it is an important determinant in your investment program. Even if you manage to pay all your bills on time, don't skip over this—a budget is a favorite topic with brokers!

You need to know what it costs you to live and how much you have left after all your fixed and variable expenses (see chart page 13) Then you can determine a budget category for investing.

Set aside *something*, even it it's only $50 a month, on a regular basis. Get into the habit. It's a good idea to save and invest at least 10 percent of your annual income. If your income is above $50,000, try to save 15 percent. The best way I know of is to take out a certain amount or percentage from your salary *before* you pay your bills. If you haven't got the heart to do it, set up an automatic savings plan at work or through your bank or credit union. Your broker, too, can do this for you. See if you can save at least 5 to 10 percent of your salary.

Look at the table below and see what happens to $1,000 when it is invested and the income earned is reinvested (or compounded) at 12 percent.

End of year 1	$1,120
2	1,250
3	1,400
4	1,570
5	1,760
6	1,970

In six years, you have nearly doubled your original $1,000. But now look at what happens over the next four years:

7	2,210
8	2,480
9	2,770
10	3,110

During the additional three and a half years, you've tripled the $1,000!

There is another bit of homework to do before you meet with a broker. It may come as a big surprise, or maybe it's something you have confidently been expecting. It is a hoped-for legacy.

Evaluating Your Possible Inheritance

If anyone in your family has promised you a little inheritance, don't count on its investment potential. Hoped-for legacies are just that, hoped for and, as Samuel Goldwyn said, "a definite maybe." There's no way you can borrow against them until they happen.

Yet legacies are indeed a legitimate part of your investment profile and belong quite rightfully in the inventory we've discussed. So if there is a possible inheritance in your future, be ready to discuss it with a broker. Know the details of how much, when, and in what form. It could alter the long-term aspects of your portfolio. For example:

Broker: Now that we've reviewed your net worth and salary expectations, have we left anything out?

You: *Well, maybe. I have a very wealthy aunt who never married, and my mother tells me that I will inherit $100,000 from her.*

Broker: How old is she—is she healthy? I don't mean to be intrusive but if there is that much coming your way in the next three to five years, we need to take it into consideration.

Determining Your Financial Goals

Establishing financial goals is like mapping out an automobile trip across the country. You need to know how much time you have, what you want to see, where you want to stop, and how much it will cost to get there.

So it is with charting your financial goals. You need to decide how much money you want to have at each major turning point in your lifetime:

- The completion of your education
- Marriage
- Buying a house
- Children's expenses and education
- Retirement

Not everyone, of course, can have their financial goals clearly in mind. Most of us are rather vague in this area because we don't take time to think it through as we should. To help a broker be effective, tell him where you want to be in a certain number of years and what you need to get there.

Without a list of goals, a broker cannot set up the proper portfolio. In fact, he may try to sell you his favorites because he is enthusiastic about them and it's easier and less time-consuming than making selections geared to meet your personal needs. By knowing your goals, *you* direct the show.

So, if you've never thought about financial goals, it is time to start. Once you've listed them, don't feel your goals are written in stone. Marriage, children, divorce, death, real estate purchases and sales—in fact, the general business of life—all add new dimensions and can change our goals. What must never change, however, is looking toward the future and devising a clear investment program.

Any time you talk to a broker, have in mind (or better still, have written down) both long- and short-term goals. He will not only find it easier to help you, but you will also win his respect.

There are three goals that belong on everyone's list, regardless of income, age, marital status, or sex:

- A small nest egg reserved for emergencies (enough to live on for six months)

- A pension plan or fixed income for retirement ($2,000 per year for a tax-deductible IRA contribution)

- A fully paid health, disability, and life insurance plan (if it is not supplied by your employer)

When you talk to a broker, tell him precisely what you already have arranged in these three areas. For example:

You: *Before we continue, I think you should know that I have a reserve savings fund of $8,000.*

Broker: Do you put money into a pension plan or IRA?

You: *No, but my firm has a fully paid pension plan.*

Broker: You should also put $2,000 per year into an IRA (Individual Retirement Account) plan. As you know, this is tax-deductible.

You: *I know you're right—I just need to be pushed.*

If you've been a little careless and you have nothing at all, tell him about it. Together you and he will find ways to fulfill the big three. Then you can move on to achieving specialized goals. Maybe some of these apply to you:

- Sufficient funds for a child's education

- Down payment for a home

- Sheltering income from taxes

- Money for near-term desires
  a new car
  a vacation home
  a boat
  travel

You will, of course, have other goals that are uniquely yours. Don't be afraid to add them to your list. Your broker cannot construct the best package without knowing all your wishes, so if you've been dying to open a bed-and-breakfast business or take a year off to bike around the world, add that to the list.

A conversation about your goals might go like this:

You: *I guess the thing that's most important to me right now is how to pay my daughter's college education. She's seven, and from what I hear tuition costs will keep climbing, so I'm very worried about it.*

Broker: I understand just how you feel, but we can set up a program combining stocks and bonds to deal with it.

As you make your list, you will notice that the amount of time set aside to realize each goal is different. Something like a vacation or a new car, which may take only one or two years, is called a near-term or short-term goal. Setting up a retirement income, which may stretch out for twenty to forty years, depending upon your age, is a long-term goal.

These time projections plus the setting and resetting of your goals provide the basis of a constructive and continuing dialogue with your broker.

SUMMARY CHECKLIST

Before you walk through the door, arm yourself with these:

- Net worth statement—including your emergency fund
- Salary—current and expected
- Amount you can save every month
- Possible inheritance
- List of financial goals

3 Investments and Personal Goals

Although it is a broker's primary job to match an appropriate investment with your personal goals, you and he can do a much better job if you learn enough about these investments to discuss them intelligently. The more you learn, the more effectively you can direct your financial future, control your destiny, and evaluate your broker's performance.

What I'd like to do is describe some of the many investment vehicles or products that are available. Then, armed with this knowledge, you can proceed with your broker to select the ones best suited for your portfolio.

Today, more than ever before, you may choose from an ever-expanding number of investment products or choices. You should know why there are so many; it will help you to understand today's financial landscape.

First, there has been a general deregulation of both banks and brokerage firms. Brokerage and banking services, which previously had been segregated by federal law, are now legally allowed to overlap. What this means is that savings banks now carry checking accounts, and commercial banks offer a wide variety of savings programs. Stock brokerage firms have banking services, including mortgages and personal loans, and commercial banks have moved into the brokerage business. The combinations of services seem endless. Many of these institutions now offer credit cards to qualified applicants.

Second, the rising federal deficit has been one of several factors contributing to a general increase in interest rates, so that banks, brokers, and savings institutions have to compete with one another for your money. They do so by offering higher rates on depositors' money and new ways for saving.

In general, then, we are witnessing a deregulated financial "free-for-all," and this is precisely why there are so many investment choices. Careful shopping among all these products will give

23

you the best return on your investment dollar.

Let me describe the basic products so that you will have a good idea of what your broker is talking about when he starts to rattle off his sales pitch.

Naturally, you might think of stocks first. We'll get to them in a moment.

The One-Stop or Central Asset Account

This all-inclusive product was pioneered in the late 1970s by Merrill Lynch, the largest full-service brokerage firm in the country. Other brokers soon followed Merrill's lead, and now nearly all the major houses and many of the small or discount ones have some type of umbrella plan. Merrill Lynch calls it the Cash Management Account, or CMA. Dean Witter Reynolds has an Active Assets Account. Prudential Bache calls theirs a Command Account, while Shearson/American Express offers the Financial Management Account. The list goes on.

Requirements to open an umbrella account vary. At Merrill Lynch you need $20,000; at E.F. Hutton, $10,000 in cash or $20,000 in marginable securities. However, at Edward D. Jones, a midwestern company, a mere $1,000 will get you started. Annual fees range from zero to $100.

Umbrella accounts provide a number of different services. This one, for example, includes:

- Day of deposit to day of withdrawal interest on your credit balance

- Checking privileges for checks with differing minimums

- A brokerage account in which you can buy stocks and borrow against them (this is called a margin account)

- Credit and personal loan services

- A credit or debit card (When you purchase a credit card you are billed for purchases and usually have thirty days in which to pay. A debit card debits or charges your account immediately.)

- The ability to wire money to any bank in one business day

- Automatic reinvestment of interest or dividends received (or they can be sent to you)

- Automatic investment plans, in which your bank account is debited monthly by a certain amount for investment in your central asset account.

- Regular monthly statements and confirmations of each transaction

- Access to the firm's research recommendations on investments

This umbrella account seems to do everything but bring you breakfast in bed!

What if you don't have $10,000 or $20,000 to open such a fancy account? You won't be left out in the cold. With amounts of money ranging from $500 and up, you can open a money market fund account with a brokerage firm. This account may not include a credit or debit card but will probably have limited check-writing privileges.

Stocks

A stock is a piece of paper signifying partial ownership in a corporation. Nowadays, a stock certificate tends to be replaced by a computer bookkeeping entry. If there were only one hundred shares of Exxon outstanding for the whole company and you owned five of them, you would own 5 percent of all oil wells, refineries, tankers, and chemical plants. (There are, in fact, 846 million shares of Exxon.)

The owner of stock has a similar fractional share in a corporation's earnings. These earnings are mostly reinvested in the company's business, but sometimes a portion of earnings is paid to stockholders in the form of dividends. For example, during 1983 Exxon paid a dividend of $3.10 per share.

Your broker may talk about *blue chip common* stocks. "Blue chip" companies are financially strong (like Exxon) with proven earnings and dividend records. (Although there are many "preferred" stocks as well, your broker is less likely to recommend these for an individual investor. See pages 121 and 123 for more information on common and preferred stocks.)

Bonds

A bond, too, is a piece of paper, signifying not ownership but debt. It is, in other words, an IOU. Bonds are issued by corporations, the U.S. Treasury, government agencies, and state and municipal governments. Most bonds have a stated (or *par*) value of $1,000. This means the corporation or government institution owes you, the bondholder, $1,000. The bond states the rate of interest payable to you as well as the date the bond will be repaid.

Thus, Sears Roebuck 10 percent corporate bonds due 2013 means that each bond will pay 10 percent or $100 in interest annually on each $1,000 bond until the year 2013, when the $1,000 principal will be repaid. The year 2013, is known as the *maturity date*. By 2013, you will have received a total of $3,900—your original loan to Sears Roebuck of $1,000 and $2,900 of interest income.

The U.S. Treasury is the largest issuer of bonds, offering maturities of ten years and over. Interest on Treasury bonds is exempt from state and local income tax, but not from federal income tax. The U.S. Treasury also issues notes—essentially a bond with a shorter maturity (two to ten years). Both notes and bonds sell in denominations of $1,000 or $5,000.

A third Treasury issue, called a bill, matures in one year or less and has a minimum denomination of $10,000. Unlike bonds or notes, Treasury bills sell for less than their full face value at maturity.

For example, if you buy a $10,000 Treasury bill due in one year, you might pay only $9,100. The difference between what you actually pay and $10,000 is your yield—in this case about 9.9 percent. At the end of the one-year period you would get back your $9,100 investment plus a $900 yield (interest)—for a total of $10,000.

Municipal Bonds

Way back in 1790, when the thirteen colonies signed the Constitution and became the United States of America, they made the newly formed federal government promise not to tax any interest that they paid to holders of state bonds. Thus was born the first tax-exempt bond. The privilege was later extended to cities and counties within each state—Philadelphia, Baltimore, Boston—and these municipalities created municipal bonds.

Today, municipal or tax-exempt bonds are a major segment of the entire bond market. States, cities, counties, and special instrumentalities of each (such as housing authorities; sewer, bridge, and road construction authorities; and so forth) issue bonds that finance vast segments of construction in the U.S.A.

After discussing your financial goals and income level, a broker will certainly suggest municipal bonds if he feels your situation requires some tax-exempt income.

Zero Coupon Bonds

This is a product that has come into being only in the last few years as banks and brokerage firms competed to attract money through innovative marketing ideas.

Zeros, as they are called, do *not* pay interest like other bonds. So why, you might well ask, would anyone buy a product that does not pay interest? Answer: Because zeros sell initially at a large discount from their eventual redemption value (or value due upon maturity). Interest is earned, but it's not paid until maturity.

For example, if you buy a $1,000 zero that matures in fifteen years and pays 11 percent interest, the discounted value (or what you pay to buy the bond) is only $200.65. To put it another way, if you buy an 11 percent zero maturing in fifteen years, you pay only $200.65 per bond, yet you will receive $1,000 at maturity, in fifteen years.

Not bad—and a good idea when you know you will need money at a certain date in the future, say for a child's education. The IRS expects you to pay tax each year on the calculated annual interest. Using the same example, the difference between $1,000 and $200.65 is $799.35. This is the amount of interest you will receive at the end of the fifteen-year period. The IRS expects you to divide $799.35 by 15 (years), which comes to $53.29 per year. This amount must be added to your annual income (even though it is not received until maturity) and taxes must be paid on it.

Zeros are therefore good for IRAs (tax-deferred) or children's accounts (where income is lower or negligible).

Here are a few recent quotations* for zero coupon bonds:

---

*L.F. Rothschild, Unterberg Towbin's Government Bond Trading Department. (Note: Quotations change daily)

To receive $1,000 in the following years, the required investment on August 3, 1984, and the present yields were:

Year of Maturity	Yield	Price You Pay (8/3/84)
5/15/1987	12.30%	$717.38
11/15/1989	12.40	529.65
11/15/1991	12.40	416.38
11/15/1998	12.40	179.37

Mutual Funds

A mutual fund is a company that uses all its money to invest in other companies—money that comes from thousands of people who pool their investment dollars together. When you buy a share of a mutual fund, you pay what is called the *net asset value* (the total value of the company's investments divided by the number of shares).

In other words, when you invest $500 or more, you become a fractional holder of this diversified portfolio. Your money is invested by professional managers who receive a fee based upon the fund's total assets. All dividends and interest income, after the fund's expenses are covered, are paid to you on a quarterly basis. The portfolio is valued each night and the net asset value per share is quoted in the newspaper.

For instance, at the close of business on a particular day, the Alliance Capital Technology Fund had a 52-week high of $23.92 and a low of $14.78. The closing net asset value for the week was $17.72, a decline during the week of 31¢. The fund had paid a dividend from income of 1¢ during the year and a distribution of $1.38 from stocks sold at a profit.

Today, there are many different mutual funds. To name just a few general categories:

- Balanced funds, which consist of stocks and bonds

- Exclusively common stock funds

- Special area stock funds for emphasis on high tech, energy, communications, precious metals, and the like

- Exclusively bond funds

- U.S. Treasury or government agency bond funds

- Municipal or tax-exempt bond funds

- Exclusively bond and note funds

Mutual funds, therefore, have two key advantages over individual stocks: diversification and professional management.

One last word, however, about costs. Many funds are no-load, which means there's no sales charge to buy in and no charge to sell. Some funds, however, charge a minimum redemption fee when you sell; others charge a sales load of as much as 8.5 percent to buy into the fund.

Money Market Mutual Funds

A money market mutual fund invests exclusively in short-term interest-producing investments.

These short-term loan instruments, which mature anywhere from fifteen days to six months, consist of:

- Discounted notes issued by the U.S. Treasury or by U.S. government agencies

- Large-denomination CDs (certificates of deposit) issued by banks—usually with minimums of $100,000 or $500,000

- Commercial paper, which are IOUs sold by large, credit-worthy corporations such as U.S. Steel and IBM

When you invest $500 or $1,000 in a money market mutual fund, you take part in this diversified portfolio. You receive interest after the fund takes out a management fee of one-half of one percent (0.50%).

These funds were originally designed for employee benefit plans and for large institutions such as corporations, schools, colleges, and churches to allow their reserve money to remain uninvested and still earn interest before they bought stocks and bonds. The idea was expanded to include individual investors.

The principal advantages of a money market fund are:

- A higher yield than is available from the average day of deposit to day of withdrawal account

- Diversification

- Professional management

Certificates of Deposit

CDs are issued by banks. They are insured by the Federal Deposit Insurance Corporation (FDIC) for up to $100,000 when the bank is a member of the FDIC (some banks are not).

CDs can be bought in varying amounts but the usual minimum is $1,000. Most carry a fixed interest rate for a stated time period (i.e., 12 percent on a six-month CD, 13 percent on a three-year CD), and these rates are well advertised by the bank. If you withdraw your money before the end of the CD period, however, you pay a penalty such as loss of 31 days' interest on CDs of a year or less and loss of 90 days' interest on CDs of more than a year).

Many brokerage firms have gone into the business of buying and selling bank-issued CDs, offering you the opportunity to prematurely unload a CD without penalty (they are paid for this very useful service by the issuing bank). When you talk about financial goals with your broker, be sure to ask if his firm offers insured CDs.

Zero coupon CDs are also available and may be especially useful for retirement planning and meeting college bills.

Your Personal Pyramid

Now that we have discussed personal financial goals and introduced some of the investment vehicles that will help you reach those goals, we can graphically structure an investment pyramid.

We start at the base of the pyramid and work up.

Level One, or the "Security Level," covers the basic necessities of financial life:

- Insurance (health, life, disability)

- An emergency cash or cash equivalent fund—savings accounts, money market fund, short-term CDs

- A retirement plan

You should have enough cash or cash equivalents to cover three to six months' worth of living expenses in case of an emergency. When you and your broker have accomplished this task, you can move on.

30

Level Two is devoted to safe, income-producing investments:

- Corporate, Treasury, and tax-exempt bonds and notes
- Zero coupon bonds
- Long-term CDs
- Buying a house

Safety should still be emphasized, but you can exchange immediate availability of money (liquidity) for higher yields. Because some of these vehicles are "timed"—that is, they will mature at a certain date—this is where a good portion of your savings program for college tuition and retirement should be.

Money for housing is slotted here, too, because real estate traditionally appreciates over time and also provides a tax shelter in the form of deductions for mortgage interest and real estate taxes.

Once you have pretty much covered life's basics—housing, food, clothing, college, and retirement—you can move on to *Level Three*. "Growth of Capital" investments are less conservative, more venturesome. Here the emphasis switches to growth common stocks. With the aid of your broker, try a mutual fund or select some specific blue chip stocks. You might enjoy participating in an investment club at this point, too.

The top level of the pyramid is devoted to the highest or riskiest of investment. You belong here *only* if you can afford to make investments that do not have a sure return:

- Stocks in new companies
- Merger candidates
- Options
- Commodities
- Index futures
- Gold and precious metals
- Tax shelters

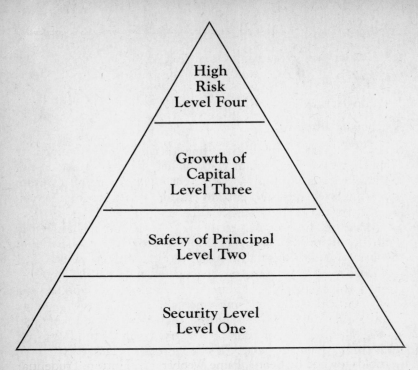

Now that you have looked at the basic investment vehicles for meeting your financial goals, and have seen where these choices fit into your investment pyramid, you are ready to meet your first broker.

4 How to Assess a Brokerage House

Selecting the right brokerage firm and knowing its strengths is an essential part of the broker hunt. The firm a broker works for influences how he does his job. The type of research a firm produces, its ability to underwrite and to spot local or regional growth companies—these factors impact heavily on a broker's effectiveness. In this chapter we will describe the major types of firms.

The Wirehouses

These large firms, sometimes called "financial supermarkets," have branch offices throughout the country. Their names are generally familiar: Merrill Lynch, Shearson/American Express, Dean Witter Reynolds (owned by Sears), Paine Webber, E.F. Hutton, Prudential Bache, Smith Barney Harris Upham, and Thomson McKinnon.

These firms compete with banks and insurance companies in their efforts to provide one-stop financial planning. Indeed, Bache & Company was acquired by Prudential Life Insurance; Shearson became Shearson/American Express; and even Sears Allstate Insurance took over Dean Witter Reynolds. This is only a partial description of an ongoing process.

Advantages of a wirehouse include extensive research facilities with the ability to closely follow hundreds of companies; a full range of financial services; complete integration of savings, checking, and brokerage accounts; an interest in handling new and small accounts; special investment plans for purchasing fractional shares of stock.

Disadvantages include an impersonal atmosphere (common to all giant organizations); the possibility that your carefully selected broker may be transferred and your account assigned to a new broker; having to work with a jack-of-all-trades broker who isn't specialized enough for your particular situation.

The Carriage Trade Houses

A specialty of New York City, these firms tend to handle investors with large accounts—six figures, that is. Some brokers with these companies, however, will take on smaller accounts. Top-of-the-liners are Morgan Stanley, Bear Stearns, Neuberger & Berman, L.F. Rothschild Unterberg Towbin, Wertheim, Donaldson Lufkin Jenrette, and C.J. Lawrence.

Advantages include excellent research facilities; brokers who are well connected with other brokers, analysts, lending institutions, and bank trust departments; high standards of personalized service; extensive investment banking activities; the opportunity to invest in new issues of stocks and bonds.

Disadvantages include lack of such services as insurance, sweep accounts, and mortgage loans; requiring a referral to open an account; preferring to deal with a wealthier clientele.

The Regionals

These houses, smaller and less diverse, follow or research fewer companies than the wirehouses but can often spot local growth stocks long before they hit Wall Street and while they are still good buys. Among the best of the regional houses are Robert W. Baird & Co., Inc. (Milwaukee); William Blair Co. (Chicago); Boettcher & Co. (Denver); Dain Bosworth, Inc. (Minneapolis); A.G. Edwards & Sons, Inc. (St. Louis); Hambrecht & Quist (San Francisco); Janney Montgomery Scott, Inc. (Philadelphia); Legg Mason Wood Walker, Inc. (Baltimore); Morgan Olmstead, Kennedy & Gardner, Inc. (Los Angeles); Mosley, Hallgarten, Estabrook Weeden Inc. (Boston); Prescott, Ball Turben (Cleveland); Rotan Mosle, Inc. (Houston).

Advantages include a more personal atmosphere generally; the ability to know the companies they follow very well; an interest in opening accounts; skill in locating new companies in their region.

Disadvantages include smaller research staffs; no nationwide network of information; the inability to offer all-in-one financial shopping.

The Specialists

These firms specialize in a single market. John Nuveen or Labenthal & Co., for example, deal only in tax-exempt bonds. There are also firms that handle only options, such as Marsh, Block & Co.

Government bond specialists include Aubrey B. Lanston & Co. and Discount Corporation of America; both companies deal only with institutions.

Advantages of tax-exempt bond specialists include an expertise in executing orders to buy and sell municipal bonds and a thorough understanding of specialization.

The major *disadvantage* is you'll rarely, if ever, be advised to buy anything but municipal bonds even when other bonds or stocks might be more appropriate to your needs.

Discount Firms

These houses execute buy-and-sell orders only—they do not offer investment advice. Commissions vary but are usually 20–60 percent lower than full-service firms. Most major cities have at least one discount firm, but if you live in a city that does not you can still trade by telephone (see page 105). For more information on how discounters work, see Chapter 13.

Evaluating the Firm

Now that you understand the different types of brokerage firms, let's figure out how to evaluate them. A good way to begin preliminary screening is by telephone.

Switchboard
Operator: Tenefrancia & Co.

You: *May I speak to one of your brokers to get some information about opening an account?*

Operator: Just a moment, please...I'm going to connect you with Mr. Bryan Beasley. May I have your name?

You: *Yes, Ray Miller.*

Broker: Bryan Beasley here. How can I help you?

You:	Hello, Mr. Beasley. My name is Ray Miller, and I'd like some information about your firm in connection with opening an account.
Broker:	What would you like to know?
You:	Well, I realize that you're a regional firm here in Indianapolis with a good reputation. But, do you take small accounts—$10,000?
Broker:	Yes, we're happy to.
You:	Do you have a money market fund?
Broker:	Yes, we do.
You:	How much is it paying?
Broker:	It currently yields 10½ percent with check writing privileges for $500 minimum per check.

While you're on the phone, you might also want to ask:

- How long has your firm been in business?

- Is the firm's research available to me?

- Does the firm have an economist or analyst?

- Does the firm handle options and commodities?

- How much does the firm charge on margin accounts? (It should be no more than 1½ percent above broker call rate. See pages 68–69.)

- Does the firm engage in underwriting new issues of stocks or bonds? Do the brokers make desirable new issues available to all customers?

- Has anyone in the firm ever been censured by an official regulatory agency?

The Role of Investment Banking

An important measure of a firm and its ability to serve your account to the utmost is its investment banking capability (its capital-raising activities). Banks and brokerage firms raise money by selling common stock for young, developing companies that wish to finance their growth by "going public."

This capability on the part of your broker may be useful to you because these new issues of stock are sometimes offered to customers at bargain prices.

Ask your stockbroker about his firm's involvement in investment banking and if new issues are going to be made available to you if you use his firm.

The Visit

Keep in mind that although many small and regional firms have merged with larger banks or insurance companies, every office still has a personality of its own. When you visit a brokerage firm, whether it's Merrill Lynch on Wall Street or Prudential Bache on Main Street, U.S.A., it can be rated by using these guidelines:

- Who are the principal partners or branch office managers, and how long have they been at this location? Rapid turnover is not a good sign.

- Do these principals engage in community activities? You want a broker and a firm who are interested in the welfare of your town.

- Are you treated courteously and in a friendly fashion as a prospective client, or does the staff seem too busy to take much time with you?

- Does the staff seem to "turn off" when they learn you are a beginning investor with modest means?

- Does the office appear neat and efficient? Is the reception room comfortable or just a place for the pizza delivery person to wait until he is paid?

- Is the person who meets with you a senior, experienced broker, or are you assigned to a young trainee? (You're not always given a choice, especially if you have a new or small account.)

PART TWO

Once You're in the Door: Interviewing and Selecting a Broker

5 Their Training and Personality

N ow it's time to learn about the stockbroker himself. Who is he? What did he do before? How was he trained?

It is the broker's job to question *you* about things like your net worth, financial goals, and budget. He has been specifically trained to learn about you. By the same token, it is your job to find out as much as you can about the broker. Your questions are not intended as a confrontation or contest of wills; rather, they should become part of the dialogue process, so that while he gains the information he needs about you, you will also be learning about him. Since you have already done your homework (see chapter 2), you will be participating in a more meaningful way. This is the essence of talking with a broker.

At the beginning of your first visit you may be asked to fill out an information form such as the one that follows.

YOUR PERSONAL STORY

A. What are your major objectives in opening an account?
_____ Capital appreciation
_____ Current income
_____ Reducing tax liability
_____ Planning for retirement
_____ Setting up a nest egg or emergency fund

B. What is your family income?

		Yours	Spouse's
_____	Salary	$_____	$_____
_____	Investments & interest income	$_____	$_____

C. What retirement plans do you have?

Company pension plan	_____	_____
IRA	_____	_____

Keogh plan   _____   _____
Other   _____   _____

D. What are your investment philosopies?
_____ Safety and long-term growth
_____ Speculative growth
_____ Income with safety
_____ Income with modest risk

E. What is your tax bracket? _____
How much did you pay in taxes last year? _____
Did you file a single or joint return? _____

F. Do you own any of the following?
_____ House
_____ Condominium
_____ Cooperative
_____ Vacation house

What is the current market value of your house?
$ _____

How much is the outstanding mortgage?
$ _____

G. What do you believe your current net worth to be?
_____ $ 15,000 to $ 30,000
_____ $ 30,000 to $ 50,000
_____ $ 50,000 to $100,000
_____ $100,000 to $200,000
_____ $200,000 to $300,000
_____ $300,000 to $400,000
_____ $400,000 to $500,000
_____ $500,000 to $750,000
_____ $_____

H. Do you have life insurance? _____ yes _____ no

	Yours	Spouse's
Number of policies	$_____	$_____
Face amount	$_____	$_____
Annual premiums	$_____	$_____
Cash value	$_____	$_____

By the time you have completed this type of form, the broker will have a great deal of information about you. Now it's your turn to learn about him.

The Next Ten Minutes

You don't need an advanced degree or great familiarity with the stock market to talk to a broker. He is the professional, but you should be a knowledgeable client. If he doesn't cover certain topics, you should. There are also some questions you should be prepared to ask.

How long have you been a broker? What was your background before entering the brokerage business? What training did you have?

These are not silly questions. The brokerage business is easy to get into. It takes only a three-month training course with a recognized member of the National Association of Securities Dealers (NASD) to become eligible to take the registered representative examination (this is long and somewhat difficult, but easy to prepare for). Once you've passed that test, you are "registered" and may sell securities.

Although I've been a stockbroker for many years, I had never been registered as a commodity broker. Recently I decided to take the training course and exam for this particular area, and in two months I had become a registered commodity broker. Need I say more?

While many accountants, MBAs, or garden-variety college graduates elect to enter the brokerage business, stockbrokers also come from a number of other areas: lawyers, ministers, well drillers, farmers, and salesmen from every field, lured by the hope of an easier and more profitable way to make a living, often find their way into the profession, especially in boom times when stocks are rising. These people often bring excellent credentials and skills to their new profession. Many large firms insist on training these new brokers for a year or more, giving them classroom experience and on-the-job training. But it is also true that there are some registered brokers who are not well trained.

It is valuable to understand a broker's background and training in order to compare him with others. Here are examples of how three brokers answered these first questions.*

Broker A: I've been a broker about eight months.... I'm twenty-seven.... Before this I worked for several other Fortune 500 companies.... I majored in engineering with a minor in business. I'm still receiving rather sophisticated training at this firm, which will prepare me to sell many advanced products.

It is fairly clear from what this young man said that he is still green and reflects the policies of his brokerage firm. If you like him, you certainly can work with him, but realize that at this stage of his career he is basically a liaison between his firm and you, between his firm's research ideas and you, the new client. However, don't be put off by his lack of experience, since in reality he may be a very capable person. If you don't want to experiment with anyone other than a proven professional, read on.

Broker B: I've been a broker twenty-five years. Went to college. Spent two years in the army. A year checking credits for a factor. Then went to the stock market. The only training I had was an informal program at a medium-sized firm in New York. I've been with this firm three years. I was at various other firms before that.

When asked why he left the previous firm, Broker B responded: "Internal disagreement."

Broker B has been in the business a long time, but we can see that his prior training was very sketchy. Being a good stockbroker requires an understanding of accounting, law, economics, and business. It would be better if he had a more academic background, and if he had gone to the New York Institute of Finance, which offers extensive courses in brokerage business, security analysis, and accounting. Brokers who live in cities other than New York can attend similar schools (correspondence courses are also available).

---

*The three brokers interviewed in this book, A, B, And C, are real people with whom actual conversations were conducted in New York City.

Here is the response given by an even more experienced broker who did indeed attend the Institute of Finance:

Broker C: I've been a broker approximately thirty years. I went to Stanford, then on to Columbia Law School, and I practiced law for five years. My on-the-job brokerage training involved going through the entire firm of D.H. Silberberg, including the back office. I also went to the New York Institute of Finance, where one of my teachers was the famous Benjamin Graham.* I got an A in Graham's course—which so startled the New York Stock Exchange that they waived the registered rep exam.

This broker obviously has all the credentials you will need. Based on this information alone, he certainly appears more qualified than the prior two; a potential investor should at this point feel quite comfortable turning to him for financial guidance.

Are you willing to work with an inexperienced client like me?

Broker A: I would. I would in fact help you to learn about the market just as I had to learn.

This is a good answer—honest and sincere. Broker A is willing to teach you, the new client—unlike an older broker, who might be impatient or condescending about your lack of knowledge. This man views working with you as a team experience and one that he would enjoy.

Broker B: I'll show you where the action is.

This experienced broker may have many good connections and sources of research, but his answer is too cryptic to tell us anything about him.

Broker C: Yes. It would take more time to work with a person who has had no experience, but I always have considered that I owe it as a service. I would prefer to

---

The dean of security analysts and author of many textbooks on stock selection and intelligent investing.

build the account of a small investor and do well for him, spending time developing the account, than take on a millionaire who is going to be much easier to handle.

Notwithstanding the fact that this broker already has an established clientele, this is the answer of a man who has a sense of the responsibility of his profession and enjoys fulfilling that responsibility. This response is clearly superior to the one given by Broker B. In addition, the wealth of this man's background and his sense of responsibility to smaller accounts make him a better choice than the inexperienced Broker A.

Another broker, Broker D, said: "Yes, I am. But it does put an added burden on both of us. I will have to take time to consult with you and you will have to listen and do some homework."

This broker may be perfectly competent and responsible, but his answer hints at a touch of impatience with newcomers to the market. Find out more about him before accepting his services.

How do you address your mistakes? Will you call me and tell me about them? If a stock drops precipitously, do you buy more or sell out? Will I be involved in the decision?

The path to successful investing is littered with mistakes, and handling them can be very tricky. Some stocks drop to half the price you paid for them and never raise their heads again. Others drop in half and then do quite well.

Your broker should know which stocks to stay with and which to dump, but sometimes overenthusiasm for a group of stocks or just plain greed will lead him to make some unfortunate choices. He should recognize his mistakes when they happen, then be ready to call you and talk about them.

Be aware, however, that today's stock markets are dominated by heavy institutional activity. These institutions (insurance companies, mutual funds, pension funds, and the like) tend to buy or sell the same stocks or industry groups at the same time, which forces their prices up or down. Sometimes stocks move in response to a single event (such as a new product or an earnings report), or as a result of an analyst's recommendation; then, everyone will sell or buy at the same time. The stock market in general—and individ-

45

ual stocks in particular—is destabilized by this herdlike institutional activity.

You may own a perfectly sound, high-quality stock that will suddenly behave in the marketplace as though it is in great financial difficulty. What may look like a big mistake on the part of your broker may only be a panic on the part of nervous institutions. If the price of stock in a sound company with strong finances declines because of this or some other condition, it might pose a good opportunity to purchase additional stock, or at least to hold on to what you have. We will see in our broker interviews how this can be addressed.

Broker A: Mistakes will always be made. Some of the responsibility is on me; some of it is on the customer. It's a matter of developing a team effort. But yes, I would call you when there's a serious mistake.

Broker B: If a stock drops 20 percent, but the fundamentals are still right and the reasons why I bought it are still in place, I like to add more to my portfolio. If something has changed or is a mistake, I'm out. I'll call you to tell you to sell.

Broker C: Assuming I don't have full discretion, I review my master list. I have a list of everybody who is invested in a given stock. I then go through that list and tell people what I'd suggest—for example, that you take the loss because it's gone sour. Then it's up to you to tell me to do it or not.

This last is certainly a fine response from a broker whose behavior and reasoning are basically sound.

What is your batting average or success ratio?

One way to assess a broker is to ask him for his success ratio or batting average in selecting stocks. Does the broker know when to play it safe and when to speculate? Are his speculations fully thought out and generally successful? And most important, does he know what percentage of your money should be invested conservatively and what percentage can be devoted to speculation? Have you and he jointly determined where you belong on the investment pyramid?

46

Assuming that this determination has been made, let's look at the answers given by Brokers A, B, and C.

Broker A: So far I've done very well, but I haven't been around long enough to have an established track record. However, the recommendations of my research department have been consistently good, and I will continue to select from their recommendations.

This answer shows us again that Broker A is sincere, but keep in mind that research recommendations in a large firm are a little shopworn by the time they get to the individual broker. Usually the salesmen who handle the big accounts—banks, insurance companies, pension funds—have first call on new research ideas. Individual brokers need to exercise their own judgment and ingenuity in using the research available to them to select successful recommendations.

Broker B: Well, if I can't get you 20 percent on your money year in and year out, I shouldn't be in the business.

You: *Is this what your track record has been?*

Broker B: Yes.

Broker B still hasn't told you how often his instincts are right, but if he can make 20 percent on a continuing basis, you should sign up with him. Before you do, though, get the names of some of his clients and check this claim out with them: Broker B may be exaggerating.

Broker C: First of all, I'd put 75 percent of your investable money into blue chip stocks, bonds, and money market instruments. Then, for the remaining 25 percent, I'd recommend some flyers in high-growth industries or technology areas. Even though one runs into a lot of price volatility in these areas, my record has been well over 50 percent. In a rising stock market it has reached as high as 80 percent.

You:	*What if I want to take more risk with my money?*
Broker C:	If you've got everything else taken care of....Have you some insurance, by the way, and an emergency fund?
You:	*Yes.*
Broker C:	Then I could increase the risk-oriented portion of your portfolio; my batting average would be about the same.

We know from our first ten minutes with these three brokers that Broker C is sound and well trained. It is interesting to note that he only claims to have a "well over 50 percent" batting average —lower than Broker B's claim, which seems exaggerated. His answer is consistent with what we know about him, which is why it is so important to spend time talking to a broker.

Will you consult with me on decision making, or will you want to have full discretion?

This is one of the most controversial areas of the brokerage business and is too complicated to cover completely. For our purposes, however, it is enough to say that a new investor should never give a broker complete discretion and should always insist on being consulted about buying and selling. Even if you say yes to everything your broker suggests, it's a good idea to have him call you to explain what he's buying, outline his expectations for the stock, bond, or other product, and discuss the risks involved in each purchase.

A discretionary account means you give your broker power of attorney to make all decisions about buying and selling. Many brokers are unwilling to accept such a heavy responsibility and insist that the final decision be made by you, based upon their recommendations. However, the process of making recommendations casts the broker in the role of "salesman," and since we know he depends for his livelihood on the commissions he generates, this type of relationship makes it difficult to know whether he sincerely likes the stock he is recommending or simply needs to make money for personal reasons. In general, the broker should be given discretion only in special cases, such as if you are out of the country, or are too busy to monitor your portfolio.

Let's see how our brokers responded to this question:

Broker A: I want to consult you on every single decision.

Broker B: I prefer discretion but don't object to discussing it.

Broker C: Later on, when we know each other better, I would prefer to have discretion. This makes it easier for me to focus on what is bought and when it is bought rather than making twenty telephone calls and explaining what and why each time.

Brokers B and C prefer to operate with at least partial if not full discretion. Stock markets move around a lot, and some decisions must be made quickly. In any event, *never* give discretion to a broker when opening an account. Only do so when you and he have known each other at least a year—and then only with the greatest discretion!

Some brokers are reluctant to deal with inexperienced clients because their ignorance burdens the selection of investment choices; in addition, such an investor is generally ill prepared to weather market loss. Other brokers (like Broker C) rise to the challenge.

There are, however, a very few unscrupulous brokers who might exploit your inexperience. This book will show you how to identify that undesirable minority.

How can I check up on you? Can you give me some references?

Broker A: You can find out about me by working with me. And I can show you some individual portfolios. Would you like to see one now?

This certainly is a forthright and honest answer. Although Broker A is inexperienced, he is open and fully cooperative. He pointed out that decisions made in the client's account result from a combination of his firm's recommendations, his presentation of them to you, and your acceptance or rejection of them; in other words, a three-pronged or team approach. He has the team approach—you, the customer; he, the broker; and his firm.

Broker B: Check with my clearing firm, the New York Stock Exchange, or the SEC (Securities and Exchange Commission) to see if there are any complaints lodged against me. And as for portfolios, I obviously will only show you the good ones.

Broker B's answer indicates a limited openness to inquiries—not a good sign.

Broker C: Yes, I certainly can give you some references. In fact, I'll show you the histories of some of my accounts. If you want to call some of these people, I can arrange that, too.

At this stage of the game, Broker C seems to be in first place, with Broker A a close second. Subsequent interviews will further clarify the matter.

By now you're ten or fifteen minutes into the interview. These introductory questions have broken the ice and given you an opportunity to evaluate the broker as a person. Whether he is open and forthright or feels he has something to hide may already be apparent. In the final analysis, selecting a broker is like selecting a doctor. You want to have confidence in that person's professional ability before you put yourself in his hands. Confidence in a broker's professionalism is paramount. Let's go on to more penetrating questions.

AVOID A BROKER WHO:

- Is patronizing or condescending
- Promises to make you rich
- Won't give you references
- Uses a lot of jargon
- Doesn't take time to discuss your financial goals or your appetite for risk
- Has changed firms three or four times in the same number of years
- Has had no previous experience and is learning with your money
- Seems poor—you don't want to hire a broker who appears down at the heels and seems not to have made a success of his own career
- Suggests you put all your money into stocks
- Deals with clients who have much more money than you
- Puts sales pressure on you to buy a product or open a certain account
- Doesn't return your phone calls
- Says he's an expert in all areas of finance
- Won't refer you to other specialists or experts

6 Finding Out How They Do Business

Does my tolerance for risk enter into your selection process?

This is a question that must be answered by every broker. If he doesn't broach the subject, you must take the initiative.

Broker A: Yes, most definitely. But you need to tell me how you feel. For instance, could you live with a stock which fluctuated sharply in price if I told you it has good growth prospects and a strong industry position?

You: *I guess I could, but I wouldn't want all my money in it.*

Broker B: Very definitely. You cut the cloth to suit the customer. I don't want any nervous Nellies around when the going gets tough.

Broker C: I regard that as a most important consideration. For example, some people are worried about taking out a mortgage on their home. Those same people are the types who shouldn't own any common stock. They should probably have nothing but treasury bills or bonds.

All three brokers answered this question in their own way but with substantially the same attitude.

Many people who open stock brokerage accounts feel they are ready to take risks—or at least that they *ought* to be ready to do so. They do not grasp the fact that the stock market can produce both gains and losses, and do not realize until their stocks drop in price just how risk-adverse they really are. At that point, unfortunately, it's too late; they blame their broker for not warning them, even for exposing them to risk in the first place.

Ask yourself these questions to help realistically determine your ability to take risks:

- Have you ever been unemployed? How did it feel? Were you scared about the future?

- Do you get frightened when making a very expensive purchase, such as a car, house, or boat?

- Do money concerns keep you awake at night?

If you answered yes to two out of the three, your risk level is low and you should explain this to your broker.

It is a good idea for broker and customer to determine exactly what percent of the account, if any, should be exposed to risk investments. Many investors tend to forget that income, growth, and safety do not come all wrapped up in one investment vehicle or package. You must be very clear about your priorities—otherwise you will be continually disappointed. If you want an investment that has the potential for making a lot of money in a short time, then you must be willing to assume the risk that goes with it.

Do you recommend individual stocks? If so, on what do you base your recommendations?

Much of the brokerage business has been absorbed by banks and insurance companies, and many of the products offered for sale by brokers either have little to do with the world of stocks and bonds or represent repackaged stock and bond products that are sold with high retail markups.

Repackaged stock and bond investments with high sales charges include:

- Municipal bond trusts
- Mutual funds with sales charges
- Zero coupon bonds

Products that have little connection with stocks include:

- Tax shelters
- Home mortgages

- Motion picture and theater investment syndications
- Life and health insurance
- Bank certificates of deposit

Many of these products are valid and appropriate recommendations. But sometimes they interfere with your direct participation in the stock and bond markets.

Let's see how individual brokers responded to this question.

Broker A: Yes, I do, but they don't make much sense unless you have a very large account. You can't buy enough of a $50 or $60 stock with only $20,000. I'd recommend a mutual fund targeted toward a high-growth area, such as our technology fund.

You: *Is that a no-load fund or is there a sales commission?*

Broker A: Well, there is a sales charge of 8½ percent.

You: *If I decide not to go into a mutual fund, how would you select individual stocks for me?*

Broker A: Our firm probably has the best research facilities in the business. I get information on about ten stocks per week sent up by the research department. These vary from the most conservative income stocks to high-growth, riskier stocks.

Note that Broker A's first effort was to sell a sales-loaded mutual fund, one that provides him with a commission. However, his firm does give him excellent backup in recommending individual stocks. Before leaping into a fund, ask for a copy of its prospectus and find out what its performance record has been over the past three to five years. Whatever you do, don't sign up on the spot before you take time to read about this and other funds.

Broker B: Yes. I select stocks based on research, knowledge, and experience.

You: *Do you do this research yourself?*

Broker B: Most of it I do myself, through friends or through brokers I play golf with. I'm also in touch with guys on the floor of the New York Stock Exchange. They keep me informed and right up-to-date.

This man could be the shabbiest and worst of brokers, or, depending upon his golf partners, he could be the best around. From your point of view, however, it is better to pick a well-trained broker, upon whose judgment you can rely—one like Broker C, who responded to the same question as follows:

Broker C: I certainly do select individual stocks, and I base my recommendations primarily on the fundamental analysis that Ben Graham taught me. However, I also tend to be a contrarian and buy stocks when the big buyers and sellers (the institutions) are getting rid of them.

Here is a sound and knowledgeable approach to stock selection. But note that Broker C doesn't say anything about his firm's research department. By now you should be comfortable and informed enough to ask about his sources of ideas and research.

YOUR BROKER'S RECOMMENDATIONS

There are many valid reasons why brokers recommend an individual stock. The following possibilities should be kept in mind when you discuss this question with your broker:

- The research department of his firm recommends it.

- The research department of another firm recommends it and through a friend or contact the broker learns about it.

- The chart of recent price movements and volume of sales indicates a period during which insiders may be buying the stock.

- A special event such as a new product, a merger proposal, or a discovery of some sort may radically change the outlook for the company's stock.

- A company's stock is selling below book value, or what its assets are worth, and represents a compelling value.

- One of the broker's customers is an executive of a company and has special insights into the strength of its sales and earnings...not insider's information, but a better understanding of the business than an outsider might have.

If the broker recommends individual stocks for his customers' portfolios, you must be ready to ask your own series of questions:

1. Does this stock meet my needs (for growth, income, long-term or short-term appreciation)?

2. Tell me about the company's fundamentals. Have the earnings per share increased over the last five years, and what are the estimated earnings for next year?

3. Does it pay a dividend? How much? Has the company been paying dividends for at least five years?

4. Is this company a leader within its industry?

5. Is this a cyclical stock or one that is recession resistant? Is it one that will suffer badly if the U.S. economy slows down?

6. Is this a mature industry or one with room for growth?

7. Do you have a research report I can read?

If your broker suggests a stock you have never heard of, ask him where it trades. Companies must meet certain standards in order to be listed on both the New York and American stock exchanges, as shown in the chart below. A stock on the AMEX is not necessarily of less value than one on the NYSE; it may merely be smaller and younger. In the Over-the-Counter Market are traded stocks of companies that range from large, well-capitalized corporations to small, highly speculative and very risky enterprises. Transactions for OTC stocks are made by telephone between brokers, whereas buy-and-sell orders are placed by brokers at the major exchanges in an auction process. Once again, however, an OTC company might prove to be an excellent investment.

REQUIREMENTS FOR LISTING ON THE:		
	NYSE	AMEX
Minimum number of individual stockholders	2,000	1,000
Minimum number of publicly held shares	1,000,000	500,000
Minimum market value of publicly held shares	$16,000,000	$3,000,000
Minimum tangible assets	$16,000,000	$4,000,000
Minimum pretax income latest year	$ 2,500,000	$ 750,000

Here is a typical conversation between an investor and a broker about an individual stock. In this case, the client knows what questions to ask.

You: *Is there any special stock you would recommend for me to purchase today?*

Broker:	Yes. I strongly recommend a company called United Technologies.
You:	*I've heard the name. Can you tell me something about it?*
Broker:	United Technologies trades on the New York Stock Exchange and is a widely diversified company, best known for the jet engines it manufactures in its Pratt & Whitney subsidiary. It has other aerospace and defense program contracts, too. However, a little more than half of the company's business is Carrier Air Conditioner, Otis Elevators, and Essex Wire and Cable.
You:	*Will this stock meet my investment goals of safety and growth?*
Broker:	I certainly believe so. Last year's earnings were $3.74 per share, and our research department is estimating around $4.40 to $4.50 this year. By next year it could move up to $4.80 or $4.90—that's a conservative estimate.
You:	*Where's it selling?*
Broker:	At $37, which is ten times last year's earnings—and we believe it will rise in price next year.
You:	*How does it rank within its industry?*
Broker:	I can't give you industry statistics because it's so diversified, but it is a leader in its key areas—defense, aerospace, jet engines.
You:	*How vulnerable is it to a recession or slowdown in the economy?*
Broker:	In the last ten years, earnings per share declined only once, from $3.53 to $3.21 a share in 1982. But it immediately rebounded to $3.74.
You:	*Sounds fine, and I'd like to buy some. Could you buy fifty shares now because I don't want to wait and then send me any research you have? After I read it, I will probably buy another fifty.*

How do you address the stock that falls below the purchase price by 10 to 20 percent or more?

Stocks can rise or fall in price and usually do both while you own them. Deep changes in the price of a stock make everyone feel sick and should be avoided if possible. Your broker should have some good answers to this critical question. Does he recheck his research sources? Is the price drop due to stock market conditions, and does the drop leave his essential reasons for buying intact?

Big losses are the cancer of the brokerage business...they exist, but no one likes them. Can your broker be counted on to minimize their occurrence? Let's look at some of the answers.

Broker A: First of all, I've never had a stock fall more than 20 percent below its purchase price. As far as a 10 to 20 percent drop, it all depends on the individual situation. Many of my stocks are long-term holdings, like IBM, GE, and Anheuser-Busch. These fluctuate with the market: if the market goes down, they're going to go down somewhat. If it's only 10 percent, I don't consider it too serious.

This man is too inexperienced to have dealt with big price drops.

Broker B: If the reasons why I bought the stock in the first place are still right, I'll use this opportunity to buy more. If something bad has happened that changes the situation, then I'm out.

Nicely put; but sometimes there isn't time to get out.

Broker C: If something went down 10 percent, I'd consider it an ordinary fluctuation. If a stock falls 20 percent, I'd look at it to see if I made a mistake or if market conditions simply took it down. I'd use this as an opportunity to buy more, but I'd certainly investigate it very carefully.

Broker C has provided us with a sound and reliable response to a difficult situation.

Here are the key reasons why stocks drop in price:

- An unexpected poor earnings report

- A broad drop in all stock prices

- Wall Street's perception that a specific industry is about to encounter lower profitability

- Declaration of bankruptcy

- Unexpected adverse developments, such as negative government regulations, lawsuits, product recalls

- Profit taking by institutional investors who feel they must sell while prices are still up.

Do you recommend bonds? How do you select them? Do you use research or simply rely upon credit ratings?

Since you have done the homework suggested in chapter 2, you now have at least a passing acquaintance with the major types of bonds, so you will understand a broker's answer to this question. But you also need to know about bond ratings. These determine the credit-worthiness of the issuing company. The stronger the issuing company, the better the rating and the lower the interest rate paid on the bonds.

There are two major rating agencies: Moody's Investors Services, Inc., and Standard & Poor's Corporation. Here is what the ratings look like:

Investment Quality	Moody's	S&P's
Top quality	Aaa	AAA
	Aa	AA
	A	A
Medium to speculative	Baa	BBB
	Ba	BB
	B	B
Poor quality	Caa	CCC
	Ca	CC
	C	C
High risk and questionable value		DDD
		DD
		D

In answer to this question, Brokers A and C said that they do indeed recommend bonds, both tax-exempt and taxable. Broker B, however, does not believe in bonds other than tax-exempt unless they are convertible into common stocks.

You should know that Broker B is expressing a long-time and rather common broker prejudice against bonds because of the inflationary environment of the last two decades.

These two conflicting points of view regarding the purchase of bonds will probably remain unresolved, as even the Federal Reserve Board regards fighting inflation as its primary task. The effectiveness of bonds hinges on the rate of inflation. If inflation rates remain at 5 percent per annum or less for the next twenty years, then bond interest rates of 12 percent or more are indeed very desirable. On the other hand, if inflation rates rise again to 8 percent, 9 percent, or more, then once seemingly high bond returns of 12 percent are far less attractive.

You cannot, therefore, evaluate a broker on his response to this question; however, a good broker will make you aware of the dilemma and where he stands.

The bond question is, in fact, a trap that may unmask a poorly trained broker. The selection of bonds, unlike the selection of stocks, is a negative art. Unlike choosing stocks, the trick is to avoid the bad ones, not find the good ones. The credit rating is your guideline. A broker will use either Standard & Poor's or Moody's ratings. If a bond is rated A, double A (AA), or triple A (AAA) by either Moody's or S&P, it is almost always okay to buy. U.S. Treasury bonds are rated AAA and are backed by the full faith and credit of the U.S. government. Exxon bonds and those of many other leading corporations are also rated AAA.

If your broker starts to talk about doing research on lower-quality bonds, such as double B (BB) or C, he is usually off base or trying to sell a product with a high retail markup. If you are a buyer of bonds, you should be seeking quality of credit rating and a fair return on your investment. If you want an investment that appreciates in value, your broker should be looking at stocks, not bonds.

Something else to consider are *hybrids*, or combinations of bonds and stocks. Convertible bonds, the most popular hybrid, can be exchanged by the owner for the common stock of the company at a fixed price at any time. They are basically another form of common stock investment with some aspects of bond protection.

How do you recommmend that I invest $10,000?

This question gets to the heart of what your broker is like. He may have a favorite stock or stocks, and you will learn about them now. He should tell you how much he wants to invest in stocks and/or bonds and how much he wants to keep in reserve, in a money market fund, for example. In any event, your broker's answer to this question will tell you how conservative or risk-oriented he tends to be.

Broker A: It all depends upon what your needs and goals are and what your tax status is. I probably could get back to you about this in a couple of days. We'd do a balance: some municipal bonds, maybe a conservative stock and one aggressive stock.

Broker B: I'd go to Italy for a month.

You: *No, seriously...*

Broker B: It's according to...well, it depends upon your investment objectives and goals. So I really can't answer until I know a rough ballpark figure of your net worth, income, tax bracket, and things like that.

Broker C: I could certainly work up a portfolio for you. But I think we should turn your investment pyramid upside down and put $7,000 at the base of the pyramid and put only $3,000 into stocks. Then divide the $7,000 between money market fund and bonds, probably a bond fund. When you have more to invest in stocks, we'll add $5,000 to that.

All the above brokers zeroed in on a key question about your theoretical $10,000—what your objectives are. Broker C's answer states it most succinctly, but they all want to know if they are handling money you need to live on or money that is surplus investable funds. All three brokers prove themselves to be ethical and responsible in their answers.

How long must I be prepared to wait to see the results of your ideas?

A really good stock selection may yield profits promptly, but this is seldom the case. Most well-selected stocks take a long time to fulfill the expectations of the security analysts who follow them. Your broker understands that to succeed in the stock market, you need the patience of a saint.

As a general rule, therefore, you should be prepared to wait one to two years to see results from your brokerage account.

Broker A: Probably you should give me a year or a year and a half.

Broker B: It's according to the investment approach. If you have an aggressive stock, you're liable to see results soon. Otherwise, one to two years.

Broker C: You will see results of some kind immediately, because you will know that part of your portfolio is returning interest or dividends at a safe, solid rate of return. For the rest, you will be in recommended growth common stocks and perhaps one or two more aggressive stocks. This portion of your portfolio may take as long as a year to show results.

All these brokers agree that you must be prepared to wait one year or longer, yet they hold out the hope that favorable results can be seen much sooner. Broker C's answer is best because he indicates he will invest part of your portfolio at a "safe, solid rate of return." You can assume from his somewhat conservative statement that Broker C won't just toss you entirely into stocks.

Understanding Speculation

In order to properly evaluate a broker's performance, it is important to focus on a key distinction—the difference between investment and speculation.

Any choice involves speculation—whether to travel by car or plane, to plant corn or soybeans, to buy Treasury bonds or conservative common stocks. In many ways, the difference between speculating and investing is illusory, because there are elements of speculation in every investment no matter how conservative—and there are elements of investment in every speculation. Most investors are unaware or choose to ignore this point and are perplexed when an investment turns out not to be 100 percent safe or 100 percent successful.

If there is little difference between investment and speculation, why, you may ask, bother to focus on this distinction? It's important because when we assess a broker's investment performance, we are to some extent evaluating his skill and track record in speculating.

Here are some typical examples of investments and speculation.

LESS SPECULATIVE INVESTMENTS	MORE SPECULATIVE INVESTMENTS
1. Keeping your money in a money market account	1. Technology and other growth industry stocks
2. Corporate and municipal bonds and U.S. Treasury notes and bonds	2. Margin trading in stocks and bonds
3. Blue chip stocks	3. Option trading

Making a Final Decision

Not surprisingly, Broker C emerges from our interviews as the leading candidate. His training and background are excellent, and he has had many years of successfully handling large and small accounts. You could rely on him to make the right decision or recommendations even in a crisis.

Broker A, contender number two, is certainly worthy of serious consideration. He is receiving excellent training from the large wirehouse for which he works, he is enthusiastic, and he is young: he will have new and different contacts within the industry, and depending upon your own age, you may feel more comfortable with him.

64

Broker B came in last in the interviews. Unless you know something specific about him from friends who have had very good experiences with him, we suggest you go with Broker A or B.

These last two requests should not be overlooked. Before you walk out the door:

You: *Would you please give me a sample portfolio of one of your accounts with the name obliterated?*

Broker: Sure. I'll have my secretary photocopy one and send it on to you.

You: *I'd also like you to include your commission schedule at the same time.*

Broker: We can actually get that for you now.

You: *Thanks very much for your time. I'll read over the material when it arrives and get back to you.*

How to Open an Account

Now that you've successfully interviewed and found a broker, it's time to open an account. In order to buy and sell securities or any of the firm's products, you must first open an account. There are two basic types of accounts: cash (the most popular) and margin. But there are still many other things to consider about your account.

Cash Accounts

Your broker will need your name, address, Social Security number, occupation, citizenship, and at least one bank reference for this standard type of account.

The New York Stock Exchange has a well-known rule: "know your customer." It means the broker is required to exercise due diligence in learning the essential facts about each customer. He will, therefore, also ask your marital status, your spouse's name and occupation, and the names of employers for both of you.

At this point your broker will ask about your financial goals and request a ballpark figure regarding your net worth.

Joint Accounts

A joint account with right of survivorship is often opened by husbands and wives. It's like a joint checking account: If one spouse dies, the other is able to sell the securities without waiting for the estate to be settled. Before you decide on this type of account, however, consult with your attorney; state laws vary widely.

Another type of joint account is called *as tenants in common*. In this situation when one of the joint tenants or holders dies, that person's half of the property goes into his or her estate (it is not owned by the other joint tenant).

Accounts for Children

All fifty states have enacted laws allowing any adult to act as a custodian without being officially appointed by a court to handle investments for a minor. This means the custodian can buy stocks as a gift for a child, sell them, and put the dividends in the child's name. Consult your accountant or lawyer for information on handling taxes and what happens if the custodian dies.

Note: Parents, relatives, or any adult can buy stock for children through a trust fund. This requires that a trust be set up through a court—an expensive and complicated arrangement, usually requiring the services of a lawyer.

Discretionary Accounts

If you are going to be out of the country or are too busy to pay close attention to your brokerage account, you may want to let your broker have "discretion" to buy and sell securities for you. To do this, you sign a *limited trading authorization*, which allows your broker to buy and sell in your account, but *not* to withdraw money.

Discretionary accounts can be very troublesome. Avoid them

unless they are absolutely necessary and revoke them as soon as possible. If you should for some reason grant your broker ongoing discretion, be certain to review the account monthly.

DISCRETION—INDISCRETION

Remember:
- Never grant discretion unless you are temporarily unable to monitor your account.
- Always revoke the trading authorization as soon as possible.
- If discretion is a permanent situation, it's smarter to find an investment adviser, bank trust department, or choose a family of mutual funds.
- Most disputes between brokers and their customers arise from the use and misuse of discretionary accounts.

Paying for Stocks and Bonds

When you place an order with your broker, neither he nor you will know exactly how much it will cost, since prices of securities go up and down all day long. When the purchase is made, the broker pays for the stock and then sends you a bill, which must be paid within five business days. Under certain circumstances—if you're out of town, for example—your broker may extend your credit an additional five days. If you have a monthly investment plan, you make your payments in advance of purchase, usually so many dollars each month.

In Street Name or Yours?

At the time you open your account, you must tell your broker whether you want your securities held in the broker's name, called *street name*, and left in his vault; or whether you want the securities registered in your name and delivered to your home or office. If you plan to have a fairly active account with several purchases and sales throughout the year, it is more convenient for both you and the broker to leave the securities in street name.

Should you decide to have certificates registered in your name, be sure to observe these four cautions:

1. Keep stock certificates in a safe place, preferably a fireproof vault.

2. Do not endorse a certificate until you sell it and bring or mail it to your broker.

3. Keep a careful record of your broker's purchase slips so you will have proof of ownership. This is especially important with bonds. Attach each slip to the bond certificate it relates to.

4. Keep an additional record of the certificate numbers in a separate place from where the certificates are stored.

AN IMPORTANT CAUTION

If the collateral in your margin account falls below the required minimum, you will be subject to a *margin maintenance call*. This means you will have to add either more cash or more securities to bring the equity minimum back up to the necessary level. If you don't do this, the broker will sell your securities to make up the difference.

Margin Accounts

The word *margin* actually refers to the part of the investment that must be paid for in cash. For example, 100 shares of XYZ Corp. may cost $70 per share. The margin rate is 50 percent, which means you need pay only $35/share or $3,500 instead of $7,000 to buy 100 shares *on margin*. (Commission, of course, is additional.)

Margin accounts can be opened instead of or in addition to a regular cash account. It means you can buy or sell securities by paying only part of their cost—the broker in effect pays the rest by loaning you the money.

The securities must remain with the broker as collateral for the loan, and you will be charged interest on a daily basis based on the *broker call rate*, which is the rate banks charge brokers for money. It is generally close to prime. Depending upon the size of the loan, a firm may charge you anywhere from ¾ to 2¼ percent more than the broker call rate.

A margin account is essentially a way to gain leverage. By borrowing, you can purchase more shares than if you paid for them in full. The potential for gain is greater—but so is the potential for loss.

Anyone may establish a margin account with a brokerage firm. A minimum deposit of $2,000 in cash or $4,000 in securities is required. The New York Stock Exchange also requires that the equity left in the account after a purchase be at least 25 percent of the current value of the stock. This is called the *minimum maintenance margin*.

A customer who opens a margin account is required to sign a margin account agreement *and* a consent to loan securities.

- *The margin account agreement* states that all securities pledged against a margin loan will be held in the broker's name for the account of the customer but will be available for the broker to use in making loans to finance other margin accounts besides your own.

- *The consent to loan securities* means that the broker has the right to loan your stock to other brokers in order to facilitate interbroker transactions, such as short selling of securities.

Types of Orders

When you open an account, you should talk to your broker about the different types of orders. It's important for you to know as much as possible about this to avoid a misunderstanding.

- A **market order** is an order to buy or sell at whatever price is immediately available (such as the going price).

- A **limit order** is one in which you or the broker establish a specific price at which you are willing to buy or sell. Your order will not be executed until your limit is reached.

- A **stop order** is an order to sell your stock if its price falls to a specified level and is used to protect investors from incurring large losses. For example, if you bought a stock at $50 and it is currently selling at $48, you might want to place a "sell stop order" at $45. This means if trading in the stock touches or drops below $45, your order is activated and becomes an order to sell "at the market." You have thereby limited your loss to around $5 per share plus commissions.

- A **term day order** is any order that is placed, since each is good until the close of the market on that day, unless it is canceled earlier. To make your order good for the week or longer, a special instruction must be given such as:
  - A **good the week** order
  - A **good the month** order
  - A **good until canceled** order

How Safe is Your Firm?

The New York Stock Exchange requires that all member firms have adequate capital reserves. This means the amount of money owed to a brokerage house (especially on margin accounts) can never be more than fifteen times the firm's capital. In fact, if the ratio exceeds 10 to 1, the Exchange can stop the firm from growing.

CAN A BROKERAGE FIRM GO UNDER?

Fifteen of them did in 1969–1970 when stock issues in which firms had invested their own capital fell sharply in price. As a result, in 1970 the Securities Investor Protection Corporation was established to protect brokers through an insurance fund derived largely from an assessment of member firms (today, all members of national securities exchanges are required to join SIPC). SIPC will advance up to $500,000 *per account* in case a member firm is forced to liquidate (cash in an account is insured up to $100,000 and securities up to $400,000).

It is still possible for a brokerage firm to go under, but now your account will be protected.

Note: For a free booklet entitled "An Explanation of the Securities Investor Protection Act," write to SIPC, 9000 17th Street N.W., Suite 800, Washington, DC 20006.

IN STREET NAME

PROS	CONS
More convenient to sell since you don't have to deliver stock certificates.	If brokerage firm is liquidated, your stock may be tied up for months.
Don't have to worry about loss of certificates or bonds. Replacement is time consuming.	When you sell, you will have to pay the firm's regular commission. There will be no discount.
If you need cash, you can get a margin loan against these securities.	
Broker may immediately invest your dividends in a money market fund; no time is lost.	
Receive monthly account of stocks' value from brokerage firm.	

Hint: If you know you are going to be selling several weeks in advance, have your shares transferred to a discount firm to save on commissions.

PART THREE
Keeping the Door Open

Do's and Don'ts of Telephone Contact

The telephone to a broker is like a hammer and nails to a carpenter. It is his lifeline, his means of contact with customers, security analysts, back office personnel, and order clerks.

The following description of his work time will help you to know when to call, when not to call, and what to expect when you do reach your broker.

Approximately 60 percent of the broker's time is devoted to direct contact with clients, usually over the telephone. Another 10 percent or more is spent overseeing the execution of your orders to ensure that you get the best possible price. In today's investment world, there are so many new and diverse securities and products that a large part of every broker's day is spent supervising the execution of orders. For example, an increasing number of quality stocks are now traded over the counter. Therefore, the broker must keep track not only of companies on the NYSE and the AMEX, but of OTC companies as well. In addition, buying and selling bonds require a surprising amount of time. It starts with a phone call to the firm's bond department to check price and availability, then a call to the customer, and then a second call to the trading desk to place the order. When the order is filled by written confirmation to the broker, he must then call his client back to confirm the transaction.

The balance of the day is divided between research and sales meetings, making sure checks are received and securities delivered —all the niggling details of the business.

You can see that the broker's day is a busy one, and his time— especially during market hours—is not his own (and perhaps not yours, either). So how can you ever get to talk with him? Should you call him or wait until he calls you? What should you do when you see your favorite stock rise or plummet ten points? To you this rise or drop in price is crucial. To him it may be one of many problems with which he must deal in the course of a normal day.

Let's see how to handle these issues. Here's what *not* to do:

11:00 A.M. Monday:

You: *Hi, George. Mel here. How's the market? How's my Atlantic Richfield?*

Broker: It's up 3.75+, and just a minute, I'll get Arco. [The broker has a sophisticated computer-based quotation machine, called a Quotron, on his desk. By pressing the right keys—in this case ARC, the NYSE symbol for Atlantic Richfield Oil Co.—the screen will print the last sale during this day's trading, the net change in price from the prior day's close, and the current bid and offer prices.]

Broker: Okay, the last sale was $54. That's up one point on the day and it's quoted $53½ bid, offered at $54. [A bid is the price a purchaser is willing to pay. An offer is the price at which a seller will sell.]

You: *Wow. That's pretty good. How about my other stocks—Chrysler and Digital Equipment?*

Broker: Chrysler is $29½, up ¼. Quote is $29⅜, ¾. DEC [the ticker symbol of Digital Equipment Corp.] is at $94¼ down a point. The quote is $94 to ½.

You: *How come Arco's up? Is there any news on it?*

Broker: I don't think there's any special news, but all the oils are stronger this morning. Exxon is up ½ and Sohio is up 1¼.

You: *While I've got you on the phone, could you explain something to me about my statement? I'm supposed to get a dividend of $60 on Arco and I think you guys must have lost it because it's not on my statement this month.*

Broker: If you'll stay on the line, Mel, I'll go to the file and get my duplicate of your statement.

Hint: While we're waiting for the broker to get the statement, we know that unless this particular client is a *very important customer*, the broker is probably getting slightly annoyed with the amount of time he is taking.

Broker: Here I am. I've got your statement in front of me and on line five of page two there is an item marked 'DIV $60 100 shares Atlantic Richfield.'

You: *Gee, I never saw that. Okay. That solves that problem. Thanks a lot. Speak to you real soon, George.*

Let's look at what this customer did wrong. First of all, he hasn't learned the art of coddling his broker. Quite the contrary, he has taken a lot of his broker's time and wasted it. Quotations can be obtained in the newspaper, and only customers giving a continuous stream of orders to buy and sell should call to ask for quotes during trading hours. And of course, no one should call on Monday morning. Monday morning is hectic because the weekend news developments have affected opening stock prices.

This customer also failed to read his statement carefully before calling with a time-consuming question. Brokerage statements can be confusing to the layperson, but questions about them should be confined to the hours before 10 A.M. or after 4 P.M. (Eastern time) in consideration of your broker's time.

Hint: You might also call your broker's assistant or secretary with this sort of question.

Here's a conversation that illustrates a more efficient use of your broker's time and capabilities.

2:30 P.M. Wednesday:

Broker: Jean Adams here.

You: *Jean, this is Bill Sullivan. I'd like to add to my position in General Motors. Can you talk to me about it now, or would you rather call me back?*

Broker: I'm just finishing up an order with the trading desk, but if you can hold, I'll be back in a few seconds.

Two minutes later:

Broker: Okay, Bill. How can I help you?

You: *I've seen the latest figures for car sales and I don't think rising interest rates are going to slow down the boom in car buying. As you know, I've got some GM, but I want to buy more. What do you think?*

Broker:	I happen to agree with you, and I'm still recommending motor stocks to my clients.
You:	*Okay. Where's it selling?*
Broker:	It's $75 to ½. Last sale was 75¼. It's unchanged.
You:	*The GM stock I own is in my cash account, but I could margin it to buy more....How about that? What's your opinion?*
Broker:	Since you own 500 shares at a lower price and they're fully paid for, you could buy up to 500 more on margin without putting up additional money. However, I don't want you to get overextended, so let's just buy another 200.
You:	*Okay. Buy me the 200 and thanks again for recommending it in the first place.*
Broker:	Shall I buy it at the market or do you want to limit your order? [see page 69.]
You:	*At the market, Jean.*
Broker:	Thanks. I'll let you know when it comes through.

This customer is far more sensitive about how to talk to his broker. He is aware of the value of time, and while he has a clear idea of what he wants to do, he also gets his broker's opinion. Consequently, as you can see, the broker responded more positively. Not everyone has such clear and specific ideas of what he wants; those who don't should ask their brokers for recommendations within the framework of their stated investment goals.

Hint: If you waste a lot of your broker's time with quotations and bookkeeping questions, you may erect a subtle barrier that will keep him from giving you his best efforts. You may never know that this barrier or negative feeling even exists, but it will nevertheless be there if you make a nuisance of yourself. Most brokers have one hundred to three hundred customers, although not all of them are active. He cannot call them all with his best ideas...and you want to be one of those he will call. Be sensitive and easygoing when you keep in touch and ask if there is anything he would specifically recommend for you. It might not hurt to take him to lunch or dinner from time to time.

- Don't call every day and ask for a lot of quotes. (It's perfectly all right to call once a week.) People who are not very busy may get into the habit of calling their broker as a daytime activity. Consult the newspaper instead, and don't let telephone calls become a recreation for you and a burden for your broker.

- Don't call to ask for explanations about your statement, confirmation, or other paperwork without first trying to figure it out yourself. Call only if necessary, and then be sure you call before or after market hours. Try asking the broker's assistant first.

- Don't tell your broker about other stocks you or your friends own, through other brokers, that are doing brilliantly. It will make him feel uncomfortable and put him on edge. If you know someone else who is doing much better, simply switch your account to that broker.

- Don't nag your broker about stock selections he made that have since dropped in price. Ask politely if he still feels the fundamentals are in place and if he is willing to hold the stock for you, and for how long.

- Don't complain that the market has gone up and your stocks have not. Instead, ask your broker if his recommendations for you have been special situations, such as takeover candidates.

- Don't take credit for good suggestions. You will improve your relationship if you praise your broker whenever possible.

- Don't ask your broker to do the research on a tip or recommendation from another person. Instead, ask him if he has any information he can contribute and, if so, to send you the material so you can make the decision. Many people feel their broker is a research library that can be put to work tracking down obscure ideas. If your broker is interested in your information, he will automatically volunteer to work on it and follow up on the idea.

- Ask your broker's secretary or assistant for help on small details about your account.

- Send articles, clippings, and any research that you feel will be of interest to your broker. Remember that you and he have a partnership that involves judgment, information, and market perceptions; it is important that you work together in these three areas.

- Call and offer praise when things go well.

- Pay for your securities promptly.

- Inform your broker of changes in address and marital status immediately.

- Tell your broker if you're going to be out of the country or unreachable for a long time so you can delegate authority to him to act in your behalf.

- Telephone if you are worried about a sharply dropping stock market. Your broker's experience and perceptions will be better than yours in a crisis.

- As you gain more experience you will be more confident about calling your broker. Meanwhile, don't be inhibited about calling him—but do be sensitive about why, when, and how often you call.

- Be certain that there is no misunderstanding when you place an order. Know precisely what you want and what type of order you are giving (see page 69). Mistakes are very costly and often are charged to the broker; they do not help your relationship.

- You may call as often as you wish to request that published information be sent to you. This type of research is readily available and can usually be sent out by a secretary.

9 Managing Your Broker

A successful relationship between client and broker is based upon mutual trust and respect. The client should understand that a broker's time is his most important asset and that commissions are the way he earns his living. A good client, therefore, will respect his broker's working time and will trust his broker to make recommendations that are suitable and not just designed to generate commissions. If that trust does not exist, the client is with the wrong broker.

On the other hand, it's the broker's job to do the same thing for you: to realize that the client's money is all-precious and must be treated properly.

In order to maintain this well-balanced relationship and receive the best possible treatment, you need to know how to manage (or "coddle") your broker under certain tense or exciting market conditions. If you make a nuisance of yourself, however, you will only put your broker off and possibly even make him start dreading your calls.

Reacting to Positive News

If an important new development occurs in a company in which you are invested, what should you do? You are certainly entitled to call your broker and ask him about it. Yours, however, will most likely be one of many calls he receives that day on the same topic, so be brief.

You: *This is Ellen Flaherty, Ed. I heard on the morning news that North Pole Oil has discovered oil in Alaska.*

Broker: That's right, Ellen. It's exciting news and they just stopped trading the stock.* It will probably open at a higher price.

Trading in a common stock is often halted when there's a major news development to give everyone time to become fully informed.

You:	*What should I do?*
Broker:	Remember, we bought it at $14½; it hit $22 before the halt in trading. I know the fundamentals pretty well and I think we should sell if it opens at $25 or better.
You:	*That's fine with me. Why don't you do that. Sell mine at $25 or better. I'm going out now, but I'll check with you after the market closes to see what happened.*

Note: Since many of this broker's customers own North Pole Oil stock, he cannot call all of them. Be sure you call him. It's also a good idea to call him if you get wind of any new discoveries or products, stock splits, takeover offers, or sharp price movements either up or down (those exceeding 15 percent).

Reacting to Negative News

Not all news is as positive as an oil discovery. When bad news breaks or when a stock drops dramatically in price (for example 10 or 15 percent), some brokers become reluctant to call their customers and discuss the matter with them. You should not hesitate to call your broker, before or after market hours, to ask about the news.

9:00 A.M.:

You:	*Ed, I just looked in the morning newspaper and was shocked to see that Eckvelt Land has dropped another three points. You told me the assets were worth over $30 a share when you recommended it at $22. What on earth is going on? Why didn't you call me or get me out?*
Broker:	Bill Eckvelt, the company president, told a meeting of security analysts four months ago that land sales were booming. Since then I guess sales have dropped. I'll call the research department and find out and get back to you soon.

Hint: Sometimes if things go badly enough, a poor broker might ignore your telephone calls completely. We hope this will not happen to you, but if it should, you have several alternatives:

- Call the branch manager or partner in charge and complain that your calls are not being returned.

- Call the broker's assistant or secretary and ask for an explanation. Why hasn't he returned your calls?

- Tell the broker's secretary when you will be home and that you will expect his call.

- Document all your phone calls. Note the time and date as well as prices of the issues being discussed.

- Read the chapter on arbitration and decide if you have a case.

The Information Revolution, Your Broker, and You

In order to better understand the sometimes amorphous statements that brokers make, you should be aware that their world changes with almost atomic speed. The more informed you are about that world, the better your rapport with a broker will be.

Today, financial information—prices and trading results, for example—travels by satellite around the world, so that banks, investment institutions, and brokers all over the world have instant access to gold trading results in Zurich, stock market trends in Tokyo, and commodity transactions in London.

This technological revolution has led to a proliferation of information—simply too much information for any one broker or investor to cope with.

This means that when you and your broker receive research information on stocks and bonds, you will both have to anticipate when something will happen before it actually does. You'll be looking at whether or not interest rates will rise or fall, whether strikes will occur or be avoided, whether new scientific breakthroughs are likely (and if they are, whether or not they will be successful). You'll need to predict new consumer trends, government regulation, and deregulation.

In such an atmosphere, the beginning investor should take refuge in quality stocks. Large well-financed companies with established markets offer the best chance for long-term success. Bear this in mind when working with your broker.

VALUE LINE

Value Line is a continually updated encyclopedia covering over 1,700 stocks. A ten-week trial subscription is $37; one year is $365. Write: Value Line, 711 Third Avenue, New York, NY 10017.

For each company that *Value Line* covers you receive a detailed discussion of the company's business, current developments, factors affecting earnings, statistical information for a ten- to fifteen-year period, short- and long-term estimates about the company's future, earnings per share, sales, profit margins, dividends, and cash flow.

Value Line also ranks each stock according to its safety and probable growth. A timeliness ranking measures whether or not the stock will outperform the market over the next twelve months. The company has a set policy regarding these timeliness rankings:

Approximately 100 companies are given a number 1
Approximately 300 companies are given a number 2
Approximately 900 companies are given a number 3
Approximately 400 companies are given a number 4
Approximately 100 companies are given a number 5

These ratings are revised weekly.

When your broker does make a recommendation and you are called upon for a decision, the first thing you should do is collect as much background material as possible. Ask him to send you copies of any written research his firm has on the stock or industry involved. (There is no charge for this service.) Then, use the local library or the firm's library to obtain data from Standard & Poor's or *Value Line*. To keep abreast of financial news in general, it pays to buy *Barron's* each week and hang on to at least the last four issues (this will tell you the price movement of any stock over the last four weeks and give you updated earnings reports for analysis).

10 If You Have a Dispute

Most brokers and most firms, as you will discover, have the client's best interests at heart. That's how they stay in business and how they maintain their reputations. No one wants trouble.

Nevertheless, brokers are human. There are times when they make mistakes. Misjudgments do occur, and a professional can be wrong.

Is there anything you can do if this happens to you? Most complaints, such as bookkeeping errors and delays in receiving stock certificates or checks, can be settled quite easily by a phone call or letter. But occasionally further action is necessary.

If you suspect your account is being churned (that is, traded too actively, thus generating excessive commissions); if you feel a broker has put you into a package or stock that directly violates your stated investment goals; or if you just think you've been cheated, there are steps you can take.

First, always write or call the broker involved and try to settle the problem agreeably. If that doesn't work, contact the branch manager of the firm by letter or by phone. For example:

You: *Peter, that new stock issue you advised me to buy three months ago has been an absolute disaster. What does Remulex do, anyway?*

Broker: They make peripheral equipment and software for minicomputers which are targeted to traveling salesmen.

You: *I bought it at $18/share and now it's down to $3½.*

Broker: I'm really sorry. Everything seems to have gone wrong with that company.

You: *When I opened my account I told you specifically I did not want to speculate! We agreed I'd invest for income with some growth.*

Broker: I remember that, but I thought Remulex was too good an opportunity to miss.

You: *But my God, you insisted I buy 200 shares!*

Broker: Well, there's nothing I can do; it's done.

You: *If you don't give me some satisfaction, I'll have to talk to your branch manager and I'm so angry I'll call a lawyer and go to the New York Stock Exchange.*

Second, if neither the broker nor his branch manager resolves the matter, you can resort to arbitration; specific procedures have been established by various exchanges to settle disputes easily.

Artful Arbitration

Whether you are arguing about $200 or $200,000, each of the major stock exchanges is required to respond to a complaint through a "uniform binding arbitration procedure." The procedure covers any member of the National Association of Security Dealers, whether or not they are a member of a securities exchange. The typical claim falls between $10,000 and $20,000 and is related to one of three problems:

- Unauthorized transactions
- Churning of an account
- Unsuitable investment program

BEFORE YOU UNDERTAKE ARBITRATION
YOU SHOULD KNOW THAT:

- Typically, the odds for an arbitration settlement in your favor are about 50–50. (In 1983, for example, the NYSE's arbitration group decided 137 cases in the client's favor and 139 for the broker.)

- Arbirtration is not the only way to settle an unresolved broker dispute, regardless of what your contract with the brokerage house states. The SEC has ruled that clients can, if they prefer, address violations of federal securities law in a court.

- If you decide to go to arbitration and the case is not decided in your favor, you cannot turn around and sue the broker. You can sue only if you do not choose arbitration first.

- One advantage of suing is that you are permitted to use discovery procedures to find other clients who may support your case.

- Act immediately if you are planning to sue or go to arbitration. Arbitrators and judges won't look favorably upon your complaint if you wait to see if the investment in question goes up in price.

Here's how arbitration works:

Step One
Call or write for the necessary forms from the director of arbitration at the appropriate exchange (see page 89) for list).

Step Two
Fill out the two necessary documents: a claim statement and a submission agreement (reproduced below).

Step Three
The exchange then sends this packet of material to the brokerage firm, which has twenty days to prepare its case. Although a firm

cannot refuse outright to cooperate, it is permitted to file a counter-claim if it believes your case is trivial or silly, such as if you lost money on a stock merely because it went down. However, if the broker promised you that its price would not fall, or if he withheld negative data, you *may* have a case.

Step Four

Before the hearing, you are allowed to reject any number of the arbitrators for "cause," but only one for "no cause." The panel will consist partially of businessmen, lawyers, and others *not* connected with an investment firm.

Step Five

If your case involves a loss of $5,000 or under, it is given "simplified" arbitration procedures. One arbitrator will read your complaint and rule based on evidence. In these small cases there is rarely a hearing. The fee is approximately $15 if handled by mail; $50 if there is a hearing.

In cases involving amounts above $5,000, a hearing will be held, probably in a city near your home. Three to five arbitrators will hear your case, and you and your lawyer can call witnesses and subpoena documents and people. So can the brokerage firm. At this level it is advisable to have a lawyer with you, since you can be certain the opposition will. Arbitration fees will depend upon the amount being disputed, but the limit is set at $550 for claims of $100,000 or more. (This does not include your lawyer's fee.)

Step Six

A decision will be mailed to you and the brokerage firm involved, usually within thirty days. The amount awarded may or may not be what you asked for; the amount is determined by the arbitrator, and the decision is final. You cannot appeal; you cannot turn around and sue. The hearing and transcripts are closed to the press and public.

Avoiding Disputes

Learning how to talk to your broker should help you avoid the kinds of misunderstandings that result in arbitration or lawsuits. But greedy and unprincipled brokers do exist, and if you are unfortunate enough to encounter one, the information in this chapter should prove useful. Keep the following points in mind during all your broker dealings:

- Never give a broker total discretion unless he has a copy of a *written* agreement stating your investment goals.

- Always keep notes on what your broker tells you (or promises you) about an investment in case there is a problem.

- Follow your monthly statements carefully; look for signs of churning (overtrading).

- Be wary of so-called insider information. Real insider information should not be available to the public, and it is illegal for a broker to use it.

- Keep in mind that the following transactions are highly risky:
  Commodities
  Buying on margin
  Buying new issues
  Buying options
  Selling short

- Never invest more than you can afford to lose in a speculative issue.

- Never put all your money in one stock or bond (except treasury bonds).

Above all, every brokerage firm has a fiduciary obligation to ensure that each investment is suitable to a client's needs and financial goals. This is the cornerstone of your right to arbitration.

For a detailed brochure on how to file for arbitration, write:

Director of Arbitration
National Association of Security Dealers
2 World Trade Center
New York, NY 10048

Director of Arbitration
New York Stock Exchange
11 Wall Street
New York, NY 10006

Hearings Department
American Stock Exchange
86 Trinity Place
New York, NY 10006

Director of Arbitration
Midwest Stock Exchange
120 South LaSalle Street
Chicago, IL 60603

Office of Consumer Affairs
Securities & Exchange Commission
450 Fifth Street N.W.
Washington, DC 20549

PART FOUR
The Inside Scoop
or
Information, Please

11 Evaluating Your Broker

Brokers and professional money managers measure their own performance against either the Dow Jones Industrial Average (DJIA) or the Standard & Poor 500 Average (S&P). You can evaluate your broker's performance, too, if you like. Here's how.

The Dow Jones Averages

For many years, the leading measurement of the stock market has been the Dow Jones Industrial Average (DJIA), which consists of thirty leading industrial corporations. The DJIA is the most popular barometer of the business, despite the fact that it's not truly representative of the whole market. The utility index is an average of prices for fifteen utilities; the transportation index represents twenty railroads, airlines, and trucking companies listed on the NYSE.

When you hear a television newscaster say, "The market rose 2 points today," or "The Dow dipped 5½ points," he is referring specifically to the Dow Jones *Industrial* Average, which is by far the most important of the four. All the averages are instantly available on your broker's desk-top quotation machine and in the daily newspaper.

Standard & Poor's Index

A number of analysts and brokers feel the DJIA is not sufficiently representative of broad market activity. For this reason, they prefer the wider-based S&P 500, which is made up of 400 leading industrial companies, and 20 transportation, 40 financial, and 40 public utilities companies.

Here's how you can use these averages to determine a broker's performance. In your monthly brokerage statement (which is usually a computerized printout), look for the column headed "Current Equity Total." This represents the financial value of everything in the account—stocks, bonds, mutual funds, money market funds, and cash—for that month. This account's current equity total can be compared with the equity total of one month ago, six months ago, or one year ago.

Thus, by measuring month-end equity for any month during the year and comparing it with December 31 of the prior year, you can determine your year-to-date progress. To simplify the process, use the following formula:

Current Equity − Equity of 12/31 prior year = Gain/Loss for Year

For Example: Current month ending Sept. 30 equity is: $17,000
minus equity for December 31, which was: −13,000
Gain for 9 months $ 4,000

$4,000 divided by $13,000 = .3076, which means you had a 31 percent gain.

Now look in *Barron's* on the page marked "Market Laboratory." Here you will find the Dow Jones Industrial Average gain or loss for the same period. In this case it was a mere 2.1 percent gain. Your account outperformed the averages, verifying the fact that you selected a good broker!

Keep in mind that personal considerations, such as your own need to maintain cash reserves in a money market fund or your appetite for risk once you reach the apex of the investment pyramid, will alter the performance percentage. If, for example, you keep 75 percent of your assets in a money market fund, you cannot blame your broker if the remaining 25 percent—invested in stocks—does not keep your whole account (100 percent) even with the pace of rising stock averages. Remember also that the two averages consist only of stocks, so compare only the stock portion of your portfolio (in this case 25 percent) with either the DJIA or the S&P 500.

Every broker (and every client) develops hunches, ideas, systems, rules, and strategies for winning the investment game. Some work; some do not. Bernard Baruch, self-made multimillionaire and financial adviser to Franklin D. Roosevelt, believed that one of the best ways to keep mistakes to a minimum is to "analyze your losses and figure out where you went wrong." Most people, including brokers, prefer to forget their mistakes and act as though they never happened. As a result, they often repeat them.

Take the time to go over your monthly brokerage statement and see where you and the broker made errors. Try to detect a pattern.

You have already been running a check of your account against the DJIA and/or the S&P 500 averages (see page 92). New let's look at the six most common mistakes brokers and investors make and see if any apply to your account:

- Not sticking to high-quality issues
- Trying to catch the minor price fluctuations of the market or of a stock
- Buying or selling on the basis of press releases about a new product or a change in earnings (security analysts try to anticipate this kind of information, so the price of the stock may already be reflecting the news).
- Clinging to a loser hoping for a turnaround
- Selling a promising stock too soon in order to take a profit
- Following the institutions

There are also some mistakes that apply only to the investors. Don't allow yourself to:

- Think that investing is easy; it isn't
- Go ahead without a long-range plan
- Stop doing your homework. Spend at least as much time researching your investments as you did buying a house or car.
- Be embarrassed at investing only a small amount. Investing only a little on a regular basis is one good way to build up a substantial portfolio.
- Spend your dividends. You should increase your portfolio size by reinvesting all dividends or interest.

The Periodic Evaluation

At least twice a year you should review the loss or gain in your account and discuss it with your broker, either on the telephone or in person (see example below). Make sure you give him time to review your account and gather the relevant information for the time period under review.

4:30 P.M. Thursday, July 16:

Broker: Well, it's nice to see you here in my office. We talk on the phone a lot, but I rarely get to see you.

You: *I know. I feel the same way and I hope reviewing my portfolio won't take too much time so we can have coffee afterward.*

Broker: I'm sure we can. I appreciate your coming in after the market closed so neither of us will be distracted.

You: *Good. Let's look at the results for the six month period ending June thirtieth.*

Broker: As you can see from this summary I've made, your account was worth $23,455 at the beginning of the year: $10,000 of this has been in the tax-exempt bond fund we bought last year and the balance was invested in three stocks and a little money market fund. Your June thirtieth statement shows the account is currently worth approximately $26,000, up $2,500. From this we must subtract the income on your bond fund—about $500—in order to get a true picture of the price appreciation of the three stocks in the account. The gain on your stock portfolio was $2,000. What do you think of the results?

You: *The $2,000 represents a 15 percent increase in the stock portion for just six months.* I checked out the S&P for the same period, and it was up 11 percent, so I think we're do-*

---

*   23,455 $13,455 divided into $2,000 = 14.89, or 15 percent
   − 10,000
   ‾‾‾‾‾‾
     13,455

	ing pretty well. How does my account look on an overall basis, including the bond fund?
Broker:	Let's see. We'll divide $2,500 by the $23,455, with which you started the year, and that comes out to 10.7 percent.
You:	*That doesn't sound so great.*
Broker:	But it's only for six months of the year. If this rate of stock appreciation continues and you add it to your fixed income from the bond fund, your portfolio will be growing at over 20 percent per year. That's more than I expect, unless this strong market continues.

This is a good example of a satisfied customer talking to his broker and receiving prompt, truthful information. Even if his account had not done so well, this broker would undoubtedly have offered concise, accurate explanations.

Not all brokers do this well for their clients. We hope you don't wind up with one who turns in a poor performance, but if you do, here's how to document it and move on gracefully to another broker.

9:15: A.M. July 30:

Broker:	Charlie Smith here.
You:	*This is Dorothy Page calling.*
Broker:	Hello, Dotty. How's everything?
You:	*Well, to be honest, I'm rather upset. I've just returned from my vacation and I looked over my June statement. It's down again. Why did you put me into stocks I've never heard of when we agreed you would stick with quality blue chips? What does Parametrics do, anyway? We never discussed that one.*
Broker:	Listen, Dotty, I wouldn't put you in anything I didn't think was good. We all run into these bad markets and we have to live through them.
You:	*I didn't realize the market was so bad, Charlie. Isn't the Dow up 5 percent? That's what I read, anyway.*

Broker:	Yes, but that's not the real measure of the market. But don't worry—I spoke to the research department about Parametrics and they're still recommending it.
You:	*A friend of mine who's a lawyer told me they're being sued by the SEC or someone.*
Broker:	Oh, that's old news. It will be settled soon.
You:	*Charlie, what can you tell me about The Flower Corporation? I bought it at $24 and yesterday it was listed in the paper at 17½ and I've got 500 shares!*
Broker:	Look, one of the firm's partners gave me some wrong information. But I hear it's a takeover candidate at this price, so let's hang on. It'll work out.

This conversation went on in the same vein for some time. Upon careful reflection Dorothy knew she had the wrong broker. She also realized part of the responsibility was hers, because she hadn't learned how to talk to her broker—he'd intimidated her from the very beginning, and her ignorance of financial matters had made her very vulnerable. It was time for a change.

How to Change Brokers Gracefully

There are three ways to change brokers. *One*, you can call the manager of the office and ask for a new broker in the same firm. *Two*, you can tell your old broker to send all your securities and cash to your home or office. *Three*, you can find a new broker and sign transfer papers at the new firm to have your old account moved over (you may or may not feel it would be polite to call your old broker first and tell him what you are doing).

Here's what we suggest:

Do Say

"Charlie, I've been dreading this call for some time, but I've decided to go to a new broker. Please don't do anything in the account as of today. But let's keep in touch and thanks for your work "; or, "I'm disappointed that things haven't worked out, Charlie, but I want to close my account. It's nothing personal, just a business decision."

Don't Say

"We're getting nowhere. I'm going to sign the transfer papers and send them to you in the morning"; or, "Charlie, send me all my stock by the end of the week," and slam the phone down; or, "I've decided to close my account. You didn't do what I wanted. Please take care of the transfer papers."

You should never completely end any professional relationship, and this applies to closing a brokerage account. No matter how angry you may be at your broker, remember that you may have to turn to him in the future for duplicate copies of statements, for tax data, or for something no one anticipates. Also, brokers talk to other brokers, and it's better for you if your old broker respects the way you terminated your account (even though it is painful to him).

Hint: If your account is worth 20 to 25 percent more than it was one year ago, don't call your broker at all...instead, send him a case of champagne and a thank-you note!

12 Profile of a Broker

What You Need to Know About Brokers

Stockbroker, registered representative, account executive, customer's man. These are the names by which the men and women who handle your account at a brokerage firm are known.

What do they do? Primarily they buy and sell securities and offer advice about an ever-expanding universe of investment products. In addition to executing buy-and-sell orders, they help customers develop broad financial goals and the strategies to meet them.

Sounds simple, but it's not. An accomplished broker must be cognizant of major economic developments, foreign currencies, domestic interest rates, and every other influence on the stock and bond markets. He must be aware of industry trends in general while reviewing the status of each specific company in which his clients have invested.

Research—
The Name of the Game

Information comes to a broker through his firm's research department and from such outside sources as:

- Economic forecasts from the firm's senior economists

- Industry trends (i.e., predictions of automobile sales and gasoline consumption)

- Individual company news and developments (i.e., changes in management, rising backlogs of orders, product price increases)

- Specific recommendations by security analysts

- Financial newspapers and magazines

- Trade publications

A stockbroker spends a considerable amount of time analyzing all this information. Often he must wait until the market closes to do his research, because during the day his time is occupied with customers and the execution of orders.

Once he has done his "homework," however, he is prepared for the next step: advising his clients.

There are certain characteristics a firm looks for when hiring stockbrokers:

- A desire to study economic trends and read research, financial, and investment material

- A willingness to spend a great deal of time doing background work that may or may not pay off immediately

- An inquisitive mind about the investment world

- The ability to make sound, sensible decisions *for other people*
- Honesty
- A joyfulness about making money for its own sake, not just for generating excess commissions.

You, too, should keep these characteristics in mind during your search for a broker.

How Does a Broker Become a Broker?

There are two basic steps to becoming a broker: on-the-job-training and the comprehensive examination.

On-the-Job-Training

To become a broker, the candidate must first be employed by a member firm of the National Association of Security Dealers (NASD). All firms who are members of the New York Stock Exchange, the American Stock Exchange, and regional exchanges are automatically members of NASD. Brokerage firms that are not members of any exchange are also often members of NASD.

Once employed, a broker usually learns the firm's operations by working in all its departments—including the "back office," where bookkeeping and securities handling takes place (today much of this is computerized).

The larger firms conduct their own academic programs in-house to accompany the candidate's on-the-job training. Typical nationwide houses, such as Merrill Lynch and E.F. Hutton, run classes year-round. Training begins in one of the firm's branch offices where the candidate was hired and consists of about 250 hours of courses structured to help the trainee pass the official registered representative broker examination.

Then the firm brings trainees from all over the country to its New York City headquarters for several weeks of sales training, during which time they learn about company research, margin accounts, investment programs, insurance, and other products. At the end of this period, they return to the branch office where they were originally hired.

Those smaller firms that do not run their own academic training program use independent schools designed to prepare brokers for the examination, such as the New York Institute of Finance and Financial Learning Systems of Minneapolis.

When on-the-job training and formal course work have been completed, the candidate is ready for the second step.

The Comprehensive Examination

The exam currently in use was developed by the New York Stock Exchange in association with the National Association of Security Dealers, various training program directors, and an independent testing firm. Given monthly, it consists of two three-hour sessions and covers:

1. Stock market operations: handling different types of orders

2. Investment banking: how corporations raise money through the sale of stocks and bonds

3. Procedures for brokerage back offices: bookkeeping, receipt and delivery of securities, and computerized record keeping

4. Investment vehicles: stocks, bonds, options, and warrants

5. Security analysis: how to analyze a company's financial statements

6. Tax consequences of securities' transactions

7. Behavioral procedures: ethical standards and government regulatory restrictions.

SAMPLE QUESTIONS FROM THE
REGISTERED REPRESENTATIVE EXAMINATION

1. **Rank the following securities in the order of priority in which they would have to be paid in the event of a corporate liquidation:**

   I. Class A common stock
   II. 4% Mortgage trust bonds due 10/1/86
   III. 6% Subordinated debentures due 6/1/83
   IV. 7% Cumulative preferred stock

   ☐ (A) I, IV, II, III   ☐ (C) II, I, III, IV
   ☐ (B) II, III, IV, I   ☐ (D) III, IV, II, I

2. **Which of the following depreciation charges cause(s) taxes to be lower in early years and higher in later years on the depreciable life of an asset?**

   I. Straight-line depreciation
   II. Double-declining-balance depreciation
   III. Sum-of-the-year's digit depreciation

   ☐ (A) III only   ☐ (C) I and II only
   ☐ (B) II and III only   ☐ (D) I, II and III

3. **A broker received the following order to sell on the opening: 1,500 U.S. steel at 51, immediate or cancel. The broker was quoted 51, 10 by 5. How many shares did the broker sell?**

   ☐ (A) 1,500   ☐ (C) 1,000
   ☐ (B)   500   ☐ (D) none

4. **The principal purchasers and sellers of federal funds are:**

   ☐ (A) Commercial   ☐ (C) Mutual savings banks
        banks
   ☐ (B) Savings   ☐ (D) Life insurance
        and loan   companies
        associations

5. **How much money would a customer be allowed to withdraw from the margin account below without incurring a NYSE minimum maintenance margin call?**

Market Value	$6,000.00
Debt Balance	3,700.00
Equity	$2,300.00

   Special Miscellaneous Account $400.00
   (Federal Regulation T=50%)

   ☐ (A) $300   ☐ (B) $400   ☐ (C) $700
   ☐ (D) The answer cannot be determined from
        the information given

Correct Answers: 1. B, **2.** B, **3.** C, **4.** A, **5.** A

(Source: New York Stock Exchange)

The Broker and You

Now that the broker has completed his on-the-job training and academic work and has passed the qualifying examination, he is officially a registered representative of the National Association of Security Dealers member firm. He can now buy and sell stocks and bonds.

And he can start earning his living from these sales. Stockbrokers are not salaried: their earnings are based on commission only, which means they make money only when they buy and sell for you, the client. This may put the broker in a position of conflict, for as a salesman he earns his living by generating commissions, but as a financial adviser, he may sometimes think it best to hold investment positions over long periods of time (during which no commissions at all are generated). So, as you can see, the broker's personal and professional ethics are extremely important. This potential conflict is also one reason we suggest that you look for a broker who is himself financially comfortable, but not so wealthy that he has lost his feeling for small accounts and people with small amounts of money to invest. Commissions rarely vary much from one full-service broker to the next; true savings can be realized, however, if you deal with a discount broker. See Chapter 13, paying particular attention to the chart on page 106.

Sometimes the best brokers generate the least commissions. This little publicized truth is fundamental to the brokerage business and should be kept in mind when you talk to a broker.

13 How to Talk to a Discounter

Should You Use Discount Brokers?

When you have reached the point where you enjoy doing your own stock selection, it is possible to save from 20 percent to 80 percent on commissions by using a discount broker. These no-frill firms will place your buy and sell orders for a great deal less than a full service broker because that's all they do. They offer few extras (although most now sell bonds and have money market funds, IRAs, and Keogh plans), no research, no individualized portfolio management, no stock or bond recommendations. No one will call you if your stocks go up or down.

Until 1975, everyone — whether independently wealthy or hard working, married or single—had to use a full-service broker such as Merrill Lynch, Prudential-Bache, E.F. Hutton, or Shearson/American Express. Then, on May 1, 1975, the Securities and Exchange Commission eliminated the price floor on brokerage commissions. The old, fixed-rate system died and the era of negotiated rates was born. Today discounters handle approximately 10 percent of the brokerage business.

How can they charge so much less than regular firms? Their service is streamlined and they basically only execute buy and sell orders. The research and decision making are left up to you, the customer.

You should use a discount broker if:

- You have investment savvy

- You enjoy following the stock market and have time to do so

- You have clear ideas about what to buy and sell, and when
- You subscribe to an investment service or serious professional financial periodicals
- You follow technical indicators (i.e., charts and graphs of price movements)
- You read professional newsletters
- You like low-priced stocks
- You have a sense of adventure
- You trade often
- You have only a one-time transaction—for example, you inherited some stock that you want to sell
- You are not afraid to make mistakes, and possibly lose money.

You should not use a discount stockbroker if:
- You cannot decide what to buy and sell
- You need investment advice
- You are too busy to follow the market
- You are nervous about things financial
- You are inexperienced.

Choosing the Right Discounter

It's not easy to wade through all the advertising hype and get to the right discount broker, but finding him could save you around 50¢ per $1.00 in commissions. In other words, if you do twelve $10,000 trades per year, you will save about $1,000 or more with a discounter.

In general, follow the same procedure for finding a discounter as you would for a full-service firm. Here are a few hints that apply in particular to picking out a discount firm:

- Get the rate/commission schedules from a number of discounters and study them carefully. Some are cheaper than others. Some have high minimums; others give commission breaks for high volume.

- Select a firm that offers just a little extra, such as a newsletter, IRA and Keogh plans, copies of *Value Line* or *Standard & Poor* research, etc.

- Call several discount firms *during* market hours. Most if not all of your business with a discounter will be done on the phone. Are your questions answered quickly and politely, or are you put on hold? Can you get stock market quotes?

- Only go with a discounter who will automatically put your idle cash into a high-yielding money market fund. You want that money to be working for you, collecting interest.

The chart below indicates the possible savings you might realize depending on which discounter you choose. Discounters' registered reps, by the way, are paid straight salaries, not commissions.

SAMPLE COMMISSIONS

LISTED STOCKS

	Full Service	Conventional Discount	Super Discount
300 @ 15	$114.68	$ 53.96	$ 40.00
800 @ 25	$357.42	$119.37	$ 73.00
1000 @ 60	$630.86	$189.14	$105.00

OTC, Assignments & Exercises

300 @ 15	$114.68	$ 53.96	$ 37.00
800 @ 25	$357.42	$119.37	$ 57.00
1000 @ 60	$630.86	$189.14	$ 65.00

Listed Options

15 @ 1½	$142.37	$ 59.93	$ 45.00
5 @ 2¼	$ 62.73	$ 39.24	$ 22.50
3 @ 5	$ 58.02	$ 41.62	$ 22.50

Discounters charge in one of two ways: according to the number of shares you trade or according to a percentage of the shares' value. You need to study the discounter's rate tables carefully and determine what kind of trader you will be.

A number of banks have entered the discount brokerage business, so check with yours and find out what they offer. To get started, here is a partial list of discount brokerage firms.

Brown & Company Securities Corp. 20 Winthrop Square Boston, MA 02110	800-392-6077 in Massachusetts 800-225-6707 outside Massachusetts
Fidelity Brokerage Services, Inc. 161 Devonshire Street Boston, MA 02110	800-882-1269 in Massachusetts 800-225-2097 outside Massachusetts
Harper-Schwerin, Inc. 936-A Beachland Blvd. Vero Beach, FL 32960	800-327-3156
Andrew Peck Associates 32 Broadway New York, NY 10004	212-363-3770 in New York 800-221-5873 outside New York
Quick & Reilly 120 Wall Street New York, NY 10005	212-943-8686 in New York 800-221-5220 outside New York
Rose & Investment Brokers Board of Trade Building Chicago, IL 60604	800-621-3700
Charles Schwab & Co., Inc. 101 Montgomery Street San Francisco, CA 94104	800-792-0988 in California 800-227-4444 outside California
Shearman Ralston, Inc. 100 Wall Street New York, NY 10005	212-248-1160 in New York 800-221-4242 outside New York

Special hint: Remember, this is primarily a telephone business. How efficiently a discounter handles your calls is important, particularly since all the discounter really does is execute your order. You certainly don't want to be kept waiting while the stock moves up or down several points.

APPENDIX

Full-Service Brokers

Adams, Harkness & Hill, Inc.
55 Court Street
Boston, MA 02108

Advest, Inc.
6 Central Row
Hartford, CT 06103

Bache Halsey Stuart Shields, Inc.
100 Gold Street
New York, NY 10038

Bateman Eichler, Hill Richards, Inc.
700 South Flower
Los Angeles, CA 90017

Bear, Stearns & Co.
55 Water Street
New York, NY 10041

Blair (William) & Co.
136 South LaSalle Street
Chicago, IL 60603

Boettcher & Co.
828 17th Street
Denver, CO 80202

Brean Murray, Foster Securities, Inc.
90 Broad Street
New York, NY 10004

Brown (Alex.) & Sons
135 East Baltimore Street
Baltimore, MD 21202

Burgess & Leith, Inc.
60 State Street
Boston, MA 02109

Butcher & Singer, Inc.
1500 Walnut Street
Philadelphia, PA 19102

Dain Bosworth, Inc.
100 Dain Tower
Minneapolis, MN 55402

Davenport & Co. of Virginia, Inc.
801 East Main Street
Richmond, VA 23211

Drexel Brunham Lambert, Inc.
60 Broad Street
New York, NY 10004

Edwards (A.G.) & Sons, Inc.
1 North Jefferson Avenue
St. Louis, MO 63103

Fahnestock & Co.
110 Wall Street
New York, NY 10005

First Albany Corp.
41 State Street
Albany, NY 12207

Glickenhaus & Co.
6 East 43rd Street
New York, NY 10017

Hambrecht & Quist
235 Montgomery Street
San Francisco, CA 94104

Herzfeld & Stern
30 Broad Street
New York NY 10004

Howard, Well, Labouisse, Friedrichs, Inc.
211 Carondelet Street
New Orleans, LA 70130

Hutton (E.F.) & Co., Inc.
1 Battery Park Plaza
New York, NY 10004

The Illinois Company
30 North LaSalle Street
Chicago, IL 60602

Institutional Equity Corp.
8235 Douglas
Dallas, TX 75225

Interstate Securities Corp.
2700 NCNB Plaza
Charlotte, NC 28280

Investment Corp. of Virginia
5 Main Plaza East
Norfolk, VA 23510

Janney Montgomery Scott, Inc.
5 Penn Center Plaza
Philadelphia, PA 19103

Johnson, Lane, Space, Smith & Co., Inc.
101 East Bay Street
Savannah, GA 31402

Johnston, Lemon & Co., Inc.
1101 Vermont Avenue N.W.
Washington, DC 20005

Jones (Edward D.) & Co.
201 Progress Parkway
Maryland Heights, MO 63043

Kidder, Peabody & Co., Inc.
10 Hanover Square
New York, NY 10005

Legg Mason Wood Walker, Inc.
7 East Redwood Street
Baltimore, MD 21203

Merrill Lynch, Pierce,
  Fenner & Smith, Inc.
1 Liberty Plaza
New York, NY 10006

The Milwaukee Co.
250 East Wisconsin Avenue
Milwaukee, WI 53202

Morgan, Keegan & Co., Inc.
2800 One Commerce Square
Memphis, TN 38103

Morgan, Olmstead, Kennedy
  & Gardner, Inc.
606 South Olive Street
Los Angeles, CA 90014

Moseley, Hallgarten, Estabrook
  Weeden, Inc.
60 State Street
Boston, MA 02109

Oppenheimer & Co., Inc.
1 New York Plaza
New York, NY 10004

Paine, Webber, Jackson & Curtis, Inc.
140 Broadway
New York, NY 10005

Parker/Hunter, Inc.
4000 United States Steel Building
Pittsburgh, PA 15219

Piper, Jaffray & Hopwood, Inc.
800 Multifoods Building
733 Marquette Avenue
Minneapolis, MN 55402

Prescott, Ball & Turben
900 National City Bank Building
Cleveland, OH 44114

Rauscher Pierce Refsnes, Inc.
2500 North Tower
Lock Box 331
Plaza of the Americas
Dallas, TX 75201

Robinson-Humphrey Co., Inc.
2 Peachtree Street
N.W. Atlanta, GA 30383

Rodman & Renshaw, Inc.
120 South LaSalle Street
Chicago, IL 60603

Roney (Wm. C.) & Co.
2 Buhl Building
Detroit, MI 48226

Rotan, Mosle, Inc.
1500 South Tower
Pennzoil Place
Houston, TX 77002

Rothschild (L.F.), Unterberg, Towbin
55 Water Street
New York, NY 10041

Shearson/American Express, Inc.
2 World Trade Center
New York, NY 10048

Siebert (Muriel) & Co., Inc.
77 Water Street
New York, NY 10005

Silberberg, Rosenthal & Co.
552 5th Avenue
New York, NY 10036

Smith Barney, Harris Upham & Co., Inc.
1345 Avenue of the Americas
New York, NY 10019

Smith, Hague & Co., Inc.
Penobscot Building
Detroit, MI 48226

Sutro & Co., Inc.
201 California Street
San Francisco, CA 94104

Thomson McKinnon Securities, Inc.
One New York Plaza
New York, NY 10004

Underwood, Neuhaus & Co., Inc.
724 Travis Street
Houston, TX 77002

Weber, Hall, Sale & Associates, Inc.
1800 LTV Tower
Dallas, TX 75201

Witter (Dean) Reynolds, Inc.
130 Liberty Street
New York, NY 10006

"Dear Shareholder," or How to Read an Annual Report

Just looking at the pictures and skimming the headlines in an annual report won't really help you evaluate the investment potential of a company, but armed with a little knowledge ahead of time, you can glean a lot of useful material from even the thinnest report.

The typical annual report consists of a letter to the stockholders from the president or chairman, a description of the company's business operations, detailed financial tables, a mass of footnotes, and a statement by an outside auditor.

It's quite easy to get lost in this forest of financial statistics, yet by developing your own search system—one that can be used with any annual report—you will soon have a basic comprehension of the business you may wish to invest in.

A word of caution: Don't let slick, glossy paper, artistic photographs, and two-tier pullouts impress you unduly. These can be merely the work of a good public relations firm and not a true measure of the company. A simple presentation of the facts and an open divulging of financial statistics are what counts.

Step One

With an annual report, it's best to start at the back and review the material presented by the auditor-certified public accountant. This generally consists of a brief statement to the effect that the financial material was prepared in accordance with "generally accepted accounting principles" (GAAP). If that's it, then the company has been given a clean bill of health. If, however, the auditor's statement contains hedge clauses such as "the results are subject to," then beware. That's accountant-eze for an unresolved problem, perhaps a legal action that carries serious financial implications for the company. Frequently it implies that a ruling against the firm may lead to lower earnings than those printed in the annual report. Some statements are even less subtle: "Uncertainties exist as to the corporation's ability to achieve future profitable operations." All auditor's reservations should be noted before reading the rest of the report.

114

Step Two

At the beginning of nearly every annual report is the president's or chairman's letter to the stockholders. Traditionally this is management's chance to comment on last year's results and the outlook for the future. It also reflects the tone and direction of the company as viewed by management. Yet you should be aware of hidden caveats here, too: "All developments went along as expected except for..." or, "We will meet our stated goals on target unless..." These are red warning signals. Approach the statement from management as an opportunity to learn how they think and plan their corporate strategies. It is an excellent introduction to any company.

Step Three

Footnotes come next. They often define terms and conditions actually used in the financial pages, such as a change in accounting methods. The footnotes will also alert you to the fact that earnings are up because of a windfall that won't occur again next year, or that legal action is pending, or that favorable foreign currency helped this year.

Step Four

After you've waded through the footnotes, turn to the income statement, usually located in the middle of the report. It will give you a good idea of what direction sales and earnings took during the year as compared with the previous year. If both earnings and sales went up during the year, it certainly is good news. It's even better if earnings rose faster than sales. The income statement also gives you a picture of the company's cash flow position. Cash flow consists of net profits plus depreciation. To arrive at a measurement of cash flow, divide the cash flow figure found in the statement by the amount of long-term debt. Anything under 20 percent is generally regarded as unsuitable—although there are exceptions.

Step Five

You should now turn to the profitability of the company. The margin of profit is determined by taking the operating income (i.e., income before payment of income tax) and dividing it by total sales. Certain industries, such as supermarket chains, have low profit margins—1 percent to 2 percent—whereas most industrial companies have margins in the neighborhood of 5 percent. Look for companies with stable and rising profit margins.

Step Six

The balance sheet, traditionally a two-page spread, contains the company's assets (everything the company owns) on the left and its liabilities (everything the company owes) on the right. Things that can quickly be converted into cash are called current assets, while the debts due within one year (which can be paid out of current assets) are called current liabilities. It is important to realize that the balance sheet offers the company's financial picture only at a single point in time. Like a snapshot, it gives you an instant idea of the corporation's strength. Its purpose is to show what the company owes and owns.

Among the things to check out on the balance sheet are:

- How much cash is included under current assets. If the amount is shrinking, you must question what is draining this money from operations. Look for a partial answer in the footnotes.

- The net working capital figure, a key number in determining a company's financial health. You can calculate this by subtracting current liabilities from current assets. This is what actually would be left over if all current debts were paid off; therefore it shows the resources available within the company to cover short-term debts. You can determine if this dollar amount is at a safe level by converting it into a ratio. Simply divide current assets by current liabilities to get the current asset-to-debt ratio. Most stock analysts like to see a 2:1 ratio. The net working captial is a crucial figure for investors to monitor, for if it drops there may not be sufficient money for expansion or future growth.

- The quick ratio, another means of determining financial strength that can be derived from the balance sheet. To arrive at this number, subtract inventories from current assets and divide by current liabilities. This figure should be more than one; in other words, current assets less inventories should at least equal if not exceed current liabilities. The quick ratio is a way to find out if a company is able to take care of its current debts as they mature.

- The company's ability to meet its obligations, another measure of financial strength. This, too, can be determined from the balance sheet by finding the debt-to-equity ratio. Divide long-term debt by total capitalization; both figures are generally given. (Total capitalization consists of long-term debt, common stock, capital surplus, retained earnings, and preferred stock.) A manufacturing company is in good shape if debt is 20 percent or less of capitalization. Higher debt ratios—40 percent to 50 percent—are acceptable in some industries, such as utilities. A high debt-to-equity ratio indicates that the company is probably borrowing to keep going—an acceptable position if sales are growing and if there is an adequate amount of cash to meet payments. Beware, however, if sales start to fall, too.

There are many more sophisticated ratios you can obtain from working with the annual report, but these six steps are a good beginning. Don't forget to look for the elementary facts, too. They're just as important and include:

- The size of the company. What are its assets? A large company is less likely to face a sudden failure.

- The age of the company. Older firms have weathered good times and bad.

- The management. Are they experienced and are they personally investing in the company?

- The company's earnings. Are net earnings per share going up? Check the previous five years' record and look for trends in net sales, too.

There are other important indicators in the annual report. So for more extensive instruction on how to make sense out of the report, write to:

Merrill Lynch Pierce Fenner & Smith, Inc.
One Liberty Plaza
New York, NY 10080

for a copy of "How to Read a Financial Report."

The important thing to keep in mind is that you must compare these key indicators from one year to the next. Is the company's net working capital up or down? What is the trend in the changes in the debt-to-equity ratio? One year's statistics are not sufficient evidence on which to judge a company.

The Proxy Statement

Second in importance only to the annual report, a corporation's proxy statement contains a large amount of useful information. Once a year, for a company's annual meeting, votes are solicited from the common shareholders to support management policies. This proxy solicitation is accompanied by a statement that contains the following:

1. A declaration by the corporate secretary as to the number of shares outstanding and entitled to vote at the annual meeting

2. The matters to be brought up at the annual meeting (usually the elections of directors, the selection of an accounting firm, changes in corporate by-laws, if any, and so on)

3. A list of officers and directors with their ages, years of service, and the number of common shares owned or controlled

4. A list of corporate officers with their salaries, retirement benefits, and the number of years before they retire

5. A list of all transactions between officers or directors and the corporation

6. A list of any lawsuits in which the corporation, its officers, and its directors are involved.

7. A list of any corporation, foundation, bank, individual, or group that is a significant holder of the common stock and may be in a position to influence corporate policy.

As you can see, the proxy statement is a veritable gold mine of information. Look it over carefully and try to learn as much as you can about the company. For example:

- Does management own enough common stock to be motivated in behalf of the stockholders, or might they only be interested in their jobs and benefits? Your own good judgment will tell you what constitutes a significant amount of stock. If the stock sells for $40–$50 per share, then 10,000–20,000 shares is a significant amount—a manager would have a vested interest in the company. If he only owns 2,000 shares, he will be far more interested in his job tenure and salary.

- Is there a large stockholder, founding family, or foundation that might want to dispose of its stock and pave the way for a takeover or merger? Any entity that controls 10 percent or more of the outstanding stock can exert an important influence.

- Are officers' salaries excessive in relation either to the corporation's earnings or the performance of the company in raising earnings and dividends? Total salaries and benefits should not exceed 10 percent of the corporation's net earnings.

- Are there significant and telltale lawsuits that point to self-dealing on the part of management?

- Are there opposing groups soliciting votes or proxies to change management or corporate policies? If a contest for your vote or proxy is going on, make sure you know which vote is in your best interest. Consult your stockbroker or go to the library to read the latest *Value Line* or Standard & Poor's report.

- Are the outside directors people of prestige and importance who may help the corporation achieve its aims of higher sales, earnings, and dividends? For example, if this is a scientific or technological company, are there any leading scientists or research professors serving on the board of directors?

Wall Street Jargon Made Easy

averages: A method of measuring broad price changes in the stock market. The Dow Jones Industrial Average is most often used for this purpose. It consists of 30 leading industrial companies listed on the New York Stock Exchange. Other well known averages include the Standard & Poor 500 and the New York Stock Exchange (NYSE) Index.

bear: Someone who believes the stock market will decline.

bear market: A market characterized by consistently lower prices.

bid & asked: At a specific point in time, the highest price a buyer is willing to pay for a stock is called the **bid**. At the same moment the lowest price at which a seller is willing to sell is called the **asked** price.

blue chip: The common stock of any very large, well known, and well financed corporation with a history of earnings and dividend stability and growth (for example, General Electric, IBM, or Exxon).

bond: A financial instrument (piece of paper or IOU) signifying debt of an issuing corporation. The bond represents an undertaking by the issuer to pay the bondholder a specified rate of interest for a specified time and then repay the debt at expiration.

book value: The total assets of a corporation less all its debt and other obligations. Dividing book value by the number of common stock shares equals the book value per share.

broker: The representative or agent of a buyer or seller of stocks or bonds. He charges a commission for his services, and is the hero of this book. A broker may be either a partner of a brokerage firm or a registered representative, in which case he is merely an employee.

bull: Someone who believes the stock market will rise.

bull market: A market characterized by consistently higher prices.

capital gain or capital loss: The profit or loss realized upon the sale of any stock or bond. A stock or bond held for six months or more and sold at a profit is taxed at the lower capital gains tax rate.

commission: The fee charged by a broker for his service as agent in buying or selling securities.

common stock: Stock representing basic ownership in a corporation, as opposed to the debt of a corporation (see **bond**).

debit balance: The amount of money loaned to an investor by a broker for the investor's margin account.

discount: The amount by which a bond will sell below its stated or par value, which is usually $1,000.

discretionary account: An account in which the broker is given legal authority by the customer to buy and sell any securities of the broker's choice at any time.

diversification: Selecting common stocks of several different companies instead of just one; mixing common stocks and bonds.

dividend: A payment made by a corporation to the holders of its common stock. It usually represents some fractional part of earnings while the balance is reinvested in the corporation. Most dividends are paid quarterly.

earnings per share: The total income of a corporation after paying all income tax, divided by the number of common shares. If the company has a preferred stock, its dividend is subtracted from earnings prior to dividing by the number of common shares.

growth stock: The stock of a corporation whose sales and earnings are growing rapidly, generally 15 percent or more annually.

institutional investor: Any large institution such as a bank, pension fund, or insurance company which invests for itself.

interest: Payment of fee made by a borrower to a lender.

investment: Using money to earn additional money through interest or dividend income and capital gains.

investment banker: A firm which buys new issues of stocks or bonds from an issuing corporation and sells them to the public.

They also redistribute already existing stock and bonds from large holders to the public.

investment company: Any corporation, company, or trust which invests in a broad list of other companies' stocks and/or bonds. A **closed-end** investment company has a fixed number of common shares which are traded between buyers and sellers like any other common stock. An **open-end** investment company is also known as a **mutual fund**. New shares are issued by the company as new buyers want to buy them.

IRA (individual retirement account): A tax-deferred account into which any wage earner may put as much as $2,000 per year from his taxable income, for his personal retirement. Taxes are paid upon withdrawal.

Keogh plan: A personal retirement program which may be set up by any self-employed individual. Annual contributions are deductable from taxable income, and taxes are paid when money is withdrawn (presumably on retirement).

liabilities:All the financial claims against a corporation. These include bills currently payable, taxes owned but not yet paid, and long-term debts such as bonds outstanding.

load: That portion of a mutual fund's selling price above the net assets per share, representing the sales commission (typically 8½ percent). A no-load mutual fund is sold at net asset value per share with no sales commission.

margin account: A securities account in which the customer buys securities by borrowing part of the purchase price from his brokerage firm. The customer's cash investment is called his margin. The amount a customer can borrow is set by the Federal Reserve Bank; currently it is 50% of the stock purchase price. (see also **debit balance**)

margin call: The demand by a brokerage firm for additional cash from a customer who has a margin loan. This only takes place when the customer's equity drops below a specified minimum.

maturity: The date on which a bond or note comes due and its face value must be paid.

money market fund: A mutual fund which invests only in high-yield, short-term money market instruments, including three-month or six-month U.S. Treasury bills, bank certificates of deposit, and commercial paper (short-term IOU's from corporations).

municipal bond: A bond issued by a state, a political subdivision of a state (such as a city or county), or agencies of states, cities, and counties. Interest on these bonds is exempt from federal income tax and from state and local tax in the issuing state.

mutual fund: An investment trust in which your investment dollars are pooled with those of hundreds of others; the combined total is invested by a professional manager in a variety of investment vehicles. (see also **investment company**)

NASD (National Association of Securities Dealers): An association of brokers and dealers in the over-the-counter stock and bond markets.

new issue: A stock or bond sold to the public for the first time by a corporation or government agency.

option: A right to buy (**call**) or sell (**put**) a certain amount of a stock at a given price (**strike price**) for a given time.

over-the-counter: The market for stocks and bonds which are not traded on the leading stock exchanges (dealers in this market operate over the telephone).

par (or face value): The amount of a bond which must be paid off at maturity (usually $1,000).

portfolio: The total holdings of an individual investor or institution in stocks and bonds.

preferred stock: A class of stock whose fixed dividend must be paid before any dividend may be paid on the common stock. If a company is liquidated the preferred stock is usually paid off after the bonds and before the common stock.

proxy: A signed authorization given by a stockholder enabling a representative to exercise the stockholder's voting right at the annual meeting.

price-earnings ratio: The ratio of the price of a share of stock to its earnings for one year. For example, a stock selling at $25 per share with earnings of $2.50 per share has a P/E ratio of 10. The P/E ratio is an easy way to compare stocks in the same business selling at different prices.

quote: Refers to stock prices. The highest price any buyer is willing to pay for a stated amount of a stock or bond at a given time is called the **bid**. Similarly, the lowest price at which any seller is willing to sell is called the **offer**. The bid and offer constitute the quote.

SEC (Securities and Exchange Commission): A government agency established in 1933 by the U.S. Congress, to protect investors and police the securities industry.

speculation: Usually implies the use of riskier investment methods such as margin buying and operating in less established, less well known stocks.

speculator: One who speculates.

street name: The name of the brokerage firm in which a stock or bond is held if it is not held in the customer's name. Stocks which are held in margin accounts must be held in street name; often customers simply prefer that their securities be held by the broker.

tax shelter: A limited partnership set up to offer tax deductions to the limited partners. Operations may be in many fields, including oil and gas exploration, real estate, farming, or movie production.

Treasuries: Notes and bonds issued by the U.S. government.

yield: The income of a security divided by its current price. For example, a $30 stock with an annual dividend of $1.50 has a 5 percent yield ($1.5 \div 30.0 = .05$).

yield to maturity: The yield on a bond adjusted for the fact that if it is selling below or above par now, it will always be paid off at par upon maturity. For example, if a bond which matures in 10 years is selling at 90, the total yield must be adjusted by the fact that the bondholder will gain 10 points over the remaining life of the bond.

zero coupon bonds: Bonds which pay no current interest but are sold at a discount from their face value; upon maturity all compounded interest is paid and the bondholder collects full face value of the bond (usually $1,000).